Why I Stand:

Boots on the Ground Against Racism

Compiled by Teresa Holmes

Edited by Ally Wharton

Table of Content

Foreword

By Robert A. Holmes Ph.D.

I am a child of segregation who experienced firsthand the realities of discrimination. I was born into poverty in Shepherdstown, West Virginia, and grew up on the "mean streets" of Harlem in New York City. I was blessed to have a grandmother who instilled in me values and moral principles that I have tried to live by. Two of the most important things that she taught me were: 1) God has blessed me so I could be a be blessing to others who are less fortunate than me, and 2) Always do the right thing and stand up for what you believe in, even if you are the only one who is willing to do so.

It is because of my grandmother that I decided as a youth to become involved in the struggle against the many injustices that I have encountered in American society. For example, at age 14, I and three other black students integrated Shepherdstown High School in 1957.

This was my first act of resistance which was the pillar that grounded my lifetime commitment to the fight against injustice. As a Georgia state legislator, I voted against the Democratic House Speaker, Tom Murphy, when he ran for re-election because he refused to appoint black legislators to be chairman of the four most powerful committees.

As Chairman of the House Committee, I battled against Republican Governor Sonny Perdue's efforts to defund programs that helped minority and disadvantaged students. Also, as Chair of the

Governmental Affairs Committee, I sponsored legislation that became law, and subsequently conformed Georgia to the National Voter Registration Act of 1993. This Act allows people to register to vote when they first get their driver's license and upon license renewal. It also permits persons to vote 45 days prior to the day of election to prevent standing in long lines on the designated election day. More than 1.5 million Georgians have taken advantage of this legislation which has helped black Georgians to increase "black political power" and make sure the black community is better represented in government.

Black people must organize and mobilize to eliminate the barriers and obstacles of the unjust system which perpetuates our oppression. We must become advocates for the oppressed and as my good friend, deceased Congressman John Lewis said, "get into good trouble." We must train and mentor the next generation so they will be able to take our struggle to a higher level. We must teach our youth the values of courage, determination, persistence and a strong work ethic so they can provide the leadership needed to be successful in our struggle.

It is imperative that those of us whom God has put in positions of authority, particularly business, education and government, become change agents and utilize their resources and influence to uplift their brothers and sisters. Jesus taught that "true" Christians must have an "active faith." He spoke truth to power, and He expects us to do the same thing.

Jesus also criticized the "hypocritical Christians," who, like todays evangelicals, talk about Jesus but never speak up or speak out against oppression, racism, injustice or any of the other evils that are prevalent in today's world. Jesus challenges us to help the poor and oppressed, to feed the hungry and care for the sick. However, those who currently have the greatest amount of political and economic power in the United States, who are in control of the United States Presidency and the Senate are doing the opposite thing. They are cutting the social services money for the poor, reducing the food stamp budget for the hungry and trying to eliminate healthcare for 130 million sick people.

Two of our greatest freedom fighters gave us words of encouragement and hope that should help us to persevere as we continue our long, arduous struggle towards liberation.

IF WE EVER GET FREE FROM ALL THE OPPRESSION AND WRONGS HEAPED UPON US, WE MUST PAY FOR ITS REMOVAL. WE MUST DO THIS BY LABOR, BY SUFFERING, BY SACRIFICE, AND IF NEEDS BE, BY OUR LIVES AND THE LIVES OF OTHERS...

Frederick Douglass

NEVER GIVE IN, NEVER GIVE UP AND NEVER GIVE OUT...

John R. Lewis

Preface

By Teresa Holmes

In the words of Ally Wharton, our editor for this anthology, "The most significant thing about every story within is that they are all super different."

Whether it is their observation of racist behavior towards others, or the neglect, explicit forms of harassment, exploitation or exclusion they have experienced personally, each contributor has chosen to raise their voices to call out racism.

What is so significant about the "Why I Stand" anthology is the diverse group of authors and team members who came together to play a role in activism.

So often, non-minorities wait for people of color to share their life experiences, trials, frustration and to come up with their own solutions, but that is not the case here. Shared are experiences and perspectives from those of different backgrounds, cultures and ethnicities.

Each one understands that this country's problem of inequity was not created by people of color and cannot be solved by people of color alone.

No Longer Silent

By Tanya Adams

Although slavery ended 155 years ago, racism, police brutality, and social injustice still exist and are undeniably present today. They may not be as visible as they once were, but people of color continue to be racially profiled and discriminated against based on the color of their skin.

As Black Americans, we tend to feel that injustice from day-to-day. We toil with the painful awareness that our brown colored skin is a visible marker to those outside of our race, making us a target for attacks and discrimination.

We live in fear wondering if one of our family members will become the next potential suspect or victim to the excessive force used by racist police officers. We struggle with the pain and anger of our oppressed ancestors, which has left unhealed scars waiting to reopen. Even in the workplace, we work harder to prove ourselves just to feel a sting of rejection as we are overlooked for promotions and remain practically non-existent in leadership roles.

Social media has become the new battle ground for a race war, as our news feeds are plagued by racial bias and discriminatory comments from people we once called our "friends."

Yes, being Black in America comes with a heavy weight and disadvantages that white people refuse to comprehend or empathize. Instead, they would rather deny racism even existed or still exists.

How could anyone turn a blind eye to the agonizing video of George Floyd, a 46-year-old black man, killed in Minneapolis by a racist police officer? "Please, I can't breathe," Mr. Floyd cried out as the white officer, Derek Chauvin, held his knee pressed against his neck for 8 minutes 46 seconds.

What America witnessed in the video footage was brutal and inhumane. It is disheartening to the Black community for anyone to try rationalizing the injustice inflicted upon him. Sadly, this is only one of the many recent racial killings, which have become all too familiar.

As a nation, we must come together in solidarity to dismantle systems that uphold racism and injustice. These systems not only insult our Black character but degrade us as human beings while presenting the false narrative that Black people pose a threat to society. To end this injustice, we need all of America, regardless of race, to stand up and advocate for equality and justice.

Our country will remain an unfair and unequal place until we address the racial problems that have manifested for years. We proclaim this to be the "land of the free" but not everyone is free. People of color are still trying to break free from the chains of oppression as we continue to fight for equal rights and justice.

How can we truly declare America the "home of the brave," if not everyone can stand up in boldness against those who keep us oppressed? Many misconstrued former National Football League quarterback Colin Kaepernick's kneeling during the national anthem in 2016 as a sign of disrespect to our country and military troops.

However, our forefathers fought for the freedom which we, Blacks, are constantly being denied. Kaepernick's actions demonstrated a peaceful protest to bring forth national awareness and change.

Our nation needs more like Colin Kaepernick, people willing to use their platforms to bring these issues to the forefront for discussion and action. We call on more prominent leaders and activists to make their presence known in the Black Lives Matter movement. We applaud singers and songwriters using their musical gifts and talent to shine light on the injustice. Even in our hometowns, we encourage organizations, politicians, and activists to champion the rights of freedom and equality for all.

This is not the time to remain silent. We must step outside our comfort zones and speak out against these wrongdoings. If we choose to remain silent, we give acceptance to the injustice against Black people. The Bible says:

> *Speak up for those who cannot speak for themselves; for the rights of all who are destitute. Speak up and judge fairly; defend the rights of the poor and needy.* Proverbs 31:8-9 - {NIV}

God provides clear direction in this bible verse, instructing us to amplify our voices for the voiceless. We not only have a responsibility as Christians but we have an obligation to each other to speak up and act against racial inequality.

I recall eight years ago, my parents went to look at vehicles. My niece was preparing for her sophomore year of college miles away and needed a reliable car to get to work and travel home during breaks.

It was a nice summer day and, although I had just given birth to a beautiful baby girl a few months earlier, I decided to ride along with them to assist with financial negotiations. My daughter was a playful baby and normally slept during car rides, so I strapped her in her car seat for the evening's adventure.

We ended up stopping at a well-known car dealership in Leesburg, Virginia. As we exited the car and started looking around the lot, a polite and professional salesman approached to assist us. Generally, I dislike being followed around while shopping but this salesman was a Black man who understood the concept of giving his customers personal space.

He allowed us to look at vehicles on our own as he took a step back, only to be present to answer questions. After looking at the cars on the lot, my niece seemed to have interest in only one vehicle. We encouraged her and my stepdad to take it on a test drive. As they drove off, my mother and I proceeded to go inside the dealership to the waiting area to keep my daughter out of the heat.

In less than 20 minutes, my niece returned to the dealership. The salesman wandered off to obtain some additional pricing information. During that time, a white lady, who I was later told worked in the finance department, approached me and uttered "aww, look at the little monkey!" gazing at my daughter in her car seat.

I assumed she must have realized immediately what she said was inappropriate because she swiftly changed the subject and began mumbling. Of course, I was stunned and speechless. For a moment, I paused as I second-guessed whether I had heard her correctly but my niece immediately confirmed what she said. This was my moment of awakening to how some privileged white people view us through their lens.

Referring to Black people as "monkeys" or "apes" has been a racist stereotype used to degrade them for centuries. It is based on past ideologies that Black people are inferior to white people, and that we share the same characteristics of monkeys.

Surely this woman had to be aware of the racial history of associating a Black person to an animal. Her remark was not only insensitive, I found it very ill-chosen to say in a workplace environment. In this situation, I felt her white privilege was reflected in her comfortability and entitlement to use a racial slur without fear of repercussions.

After bringing the incident to our salesman's attention, he went to the back to speak directly to his colleague. Upon his return, he attempted to smooth things over by expressing his own apology and stating he did not think she meant the term in a negative way. At that point, I was already angry as she lacked the common courtesy to come apologize face to face.

I glanced over at my mother. I could tell she was a little unnerved not knowing how I would respond. I have always been the outspoken member of my family and my words and actions have not always aligned with my mother's Christian way. However, standing up for what is right had become an integral part of who I was, and I could not allow the employee's racial ignorance to be swept under the rug. Choosing not to cause a scene in front of my parents was a difficult decision. Nevertheless, I had come to the realization that Black people are often perceived as aggressors in incidents involving race.

I knew I needed time to process my emotions to respond meaningfully rather than react quickly. I politely thanked the salesman for his time and further explained my family would not be doing business with his dealership.

The next morning, I contacted senior management at the car dealership to ensure the incident was reported. Although I felt the manager's apology was sincere, I was still annoyed by the company not having the employee apologize directly to me. The manager assured me the matter would be addressed with the employee but I was not fully convinced. At the very least, I knew confronting the incident brought awareness to the history of "monkey" stereotyping and would cause her to choose her words more carefully in the future.

How often are we asked to remain silent and not make a big deal out of "little things?" Most Black Americans will attest that racism and racial injustice are not little things and we believe them to be major concerns in our nation.

As Dr. Martin Luther King, Jr. once stated: "Our lives begin to end the day we become silent about things that matter."

Equality matters. Justice matters. Freedom matters. Rayshard Brooks, George Floyd, Breonna Taylor, Ahmaud Arbery, Stephon Clark, Botham Jean, Philando Castille, Alton Sterling, Freddie Gray, Eric Garner, and Trayvon Martin are among the many Black lives that mattered.

As tension continues to fuel amongst races, the recent killing of a 5-year old white boy, Cannon Hinnant, in North Carolina has sparked a new racial controversy. Many are blaming the Black Lives Matter movement for the lack of media coverage provided on Cannon's murder compared to the national coverage given to the George Floyd case. People are asking: "Where is the national news coverage?" "Where is the outrage?" and "Where is the rioting and looting for Cannon?"

The fact is, Black Lives Matter has no control over the news outlets. Both incidents were senseless acts of violence but to compare them shows how insensitive our world has become exploiting one's own racist agenda.

Unlike the George Floyd case, the suspect in Cannon's shooting was arrested within 24 hours of the crime. There was no live video necessary to force law enforcement to make an arrest. It is repulsive to see folks using the tragic death of Cannon as a way to discredit the Black Lives Matter Movement by portraying the organization as hypocritical and suggesting that we do not care about this precious boy's death because he was white and the suspect was a Black man.

Yet here we are. This was a horrible tragedy. The color of skin becomes irrelevant when it comes to an innocent child being shot to death while riding his bicycle. I can only imagine most parents felt some sense of emotion hearing the news of Cannon's death, whether we knew him directly or not. Just to be clear, Cannon Hinnant's life mattered!

Until we start addressing racial issues and dealing with the ways in which injustice and inequality rear their ugly heads into our businesses and society, our country will never progress. No longer can we turn a blind eye. Each of us must take responsibility in becoming a part of the solution to bring change and to address the underlying conditions and causes of racism and injustice.

Ultimately, we remain hopeful. Despite the recent tragedies, our nation will continue to strive for ways to right the wrongs of our past, and promote a culture of inclusion, so all people feel accepted, heard, and treated equally.

Together we can build a strong nation that advocates for the human rights of all people, that not only values their lives but protects them too.

It's About Them

By Asa "Lovechild" Arnold

My activist journey began early in my life. One could almost say I was born into it. The rebel in me came to the surface when I was eight years old. My mother was a schoolteacher and kept me close to her at all times. Wherever she was teaching, I was enrolled.

Third grade was the first time I was not at the same school as my mother.

The added layer of protection from being with her all the time was gone but my independence was intact. I was ready to take on the world in my pixie dress, glasses, and my curly top hair. That was, until a little white girl stepped on my foot in the school lunch line, raised her hand, and told the teacher that I stepped on her foot.

Without batting an eye or hearing a word I said in self-defense, the teacher reprimanded me to the back of the line. It was at that point I knew I was different. I sadly, with my head bowed low, took my punishment and slowly walked to the back of the line. I was the last to eat that day and swore from that day forward that I would not be the last to eat ever again.

It's funny that memory is a mainstay after all of these years. I don't know if it was an instinct or me coming to grips with having to be cautious at all times of how I moved and who I talked to and befriended.

From that point on, whenever I got in trouble in school, which was rare, it was because I was standing up for another young Black girl because I did not want to see anyone being treated unfairly.

My dance coach in high school had the girls on the team raise money for new outfits and a new tape recorder. When the time came for us to see the fruits of our labor, our coach had no explanation and told us it did not matter.

I was not having it and proceeded to boycott. My efforts to get what our coach owed us landed me in the principal's office. As principals go, nothing varies from script, so the first obvious threat was to call my mother.

She never said she would call my father, but always threatened to call my mother, which in hindsight is strange to me. Why not ask to speak with both of my parents? I remember very clearly both of my parents showing up for the conference with the principal, who insisted I wait outside of the office. Little did the principal know, after the disagreement with the coach, I immediately told my parents the evening before her conference with them the next day.

The outcome was not in my favor but my parents were grateful I was not afraid to confront the situation and not afraid to go to them when something went wrong.

The next week, the principal saw me in the lunchroom and decided to ask me if I was behaving, as though I was her child. I gave her a death stare and waited for her to get the hint to walk away. It was not that I did not want to answer her, it was the way she spoke to me. I felt like she was taking advantage of her authority to make me feel like I had lost a world war and that my place was to be seen but not heard. Rather than disrespect her as I felt she did me, I tried my best to hold my tongue. I went down the hall and let my frustration out by beating the hell out of someone's locker. I felt muted with no outlet.

The third grade was also around the time my personal identity of what it meant to be Black in America began to take shape. I am unsure if my mother just saw the need to educate me more or if she realized I was coming into an age where I was becoming more aware of what type of people, places, and things I saw.

My mother started igniting my expression through the creative arts. I started learning different genres of African and street dance, took up the violin, acted in the only Black owned theatre company in my town, sang in local talent shows, and participated in music camps at one of the downtown YMCAs.

I read a lot, as one of my older brothers would drag me along to one of the only African American bookstores in town. I am from the small town of Louisville, Kentucky and although it was unspoken growing up, there was definitely a difference between the Black side of town and the white side of town.

My mother and father purposely laid their foundation in the east end of town because in their eyes the east end provided me and my brothers a better way of life. I quickly learned that although there was easy access to opportunity, getting those opportunities would be equally hard no matter where I grew up. The bottom line was that my skin was Black.

The color divide was very clear. If you were anything other than white, you were Black. It did not matter what country or ethnic background you represented; you were Black in Kentucky if you had any drop of color in you at all.

I remember being intrigued by what my brother was reading or what event he was attending for a Black cause on the campus of the college he went. He always got stuck taking care of me while my mother was working in the evenings, so by default I was at his hip for most of his outings on campus.

By the time I was 12, I had completed books such as *Black Power, The Isis Papers, Autobiography of Malcolm X.* I also learned that my mother, father, and stepfather were all involved in the Civil Rights Movement from early ages, in their respective states of Kentucky and North Carolina. The pride I took in just knowing that as a teenager was special to me. I walked with my chest out and chin up.

My generation saw hip-hop find its own voice and within that I felt strong enough to use mine.

My examples were fierce. I saw myself everywhere I turned, mainly because my mother kept positive Black imagery in front of me. I also grew up at a time when rappers were making a point to talk about the Black agenda and the psychological betterment of our communities.

I grew up listening to Public Enemy, Queen Latifah, XClan, Monie Love, Boogie Down Productions, and their equals so the blueprint was there for me to follow. Just off the strength of music alone, I felt like I could do anything and deserved to walk with pride. I was on top of the world as a teenager. However, by the time I was 15 and coming of age, things changed. My older brother and I were pulled over in the suburbs about three miles from our house for running a red light. My brother pulled over and got out of the car as instructed. Immediately, I was told to step aside as they patted my brother down.

Then it was my turn, after waiting for a female officer to arrive. She patted me down and I remember her asking me repeatedly in different ways if I had any drugs on me, to which I replied no.

At that point, my brother mentioned that my uncle was a major on the police force. It was only then that they stopped asking questions and waited for our parents to arrive.

It was as if my uncle was Midas. I was relieved but knew because of past trauma from experiencing the mind games people in power play, the outcome could have been worse. I honestly believe if we did not say anything about our uncle, we would have gone to jail.

As a Black person, for me, there is no difference between being discriminated against in a predominantly Black neighborhood and a predominantly white neighborhood. Being Black in a predominantly Black neighborhood, you are treated like you are an animal in a cage by those in power. On the other hand, when you are Black in a predominantly white neighborhood the powers that be treat you as if you are trespassing.

In either environment, those more privileged than others feel they have the right to dictate how you are to live and exist.

The slave mentality has not changed. All these experiences throughout my life have shaped my attitude about the state of the world and predicaments that as Black people we find ourselves in still today.

The only thing that has changed for us is time. The patterns and the behavior of those that are in power is the same as it was when my parents fought for my right to sit on a bus or walk in the front door of a business. The faces may be different but their perception and preconceived notions remain.

I did not choose to fight for others, standing up for others chose me. I stood then as I do now. Many of us have not stopped fighting since birth. Standing up for the rights of black people is a torch passed down to us by default. You either stand or you die trying, and if you can't then stand back and let others do what they must.

For a while, the racism and injustice that we faced was subliminal at best. Most of us were all going about our daily lives unaware that there were hidden injustices that went on underneath. There was no technology to expose the behavior, so these injustices remained unproven and continued to gain momentum underground.

On a hot fateful day on August 9th, 2014, the nation turned on its head after Michael Brown's body was left in the street for hours, uncovered and leaving a community reeling and a nation of Black people wanting answers.

The hearts of Black folks sank as sadness, rage, and anger played out on national television. I felt helpless. It seemed like the racism that was always there received a second wind. The summer heated up and there were even more injustices against Black people. It was like a never-ending wheel of pain. I felt numb and remembered the same feeling from growing up. The pain never stopped, it just transferred to the next generation.

Now the cycle repeats itself. People are left wondering what to do. *How do I fight? How do I as a member of the generation before help?*

I found the answer.

You start right where you physically are. We are all activists in our own right as the same injustices happen in all our own backyards and are seen on repeat through the news and social media. I chose to continue what was already in me. It starts with my voice. I made the decision to continue to help by being unapologetically vocal about the injustices that continue to plague my people.

Why do I stand? I stand because my parents stood for me, I had to stand for myself, and now unfortunately the same exact injustices are continuing to rear their ugly head with our children.

I stand for the generations that come after me and the generations before me who took the physical blows, insults, frustrations, and tragedies for me to live. I choose to stand because the trauma embedded in us all is triggered by a never-ending wash, rinse, repeat cycle that must find resolve.

Silent No More

By Laura Beard

I have tried many times to put my feelings on the current state of our world and our country into words. I have struggled with it for years. I am astounded by the lack of understanding and respect white people have for people of other races. I am white. I am a mother to five bi-racial (Black/white) children: two boys and three girls. My grandsons are bi-racial and my granddaughter is Black, white, and Mexican. For me, to say I don't see color would be a lie.

I pray I will always see color, culture, ethnicity, and celebrate the beauty of it all, treating people equally and with dignity. Diversity is not something to be feared but something to be enjoyed. There is beauty in it like the brightness of the sun on a warm, sunny day or the pounding sound of rain on the roof during a storm. You have to see it and listen to it before you can begin to understand it.

My children have grown up in a home that embraces Black culture. The music they listen to, the food they eat, and their sense of style, have all been influenced by their Black culture. My husband and I have set standards for our children and they have exceeded them even more than I could have imagined.

Our children have done well academically and athletically but still struggle to find their place in the small, predominantly white town where we live. Through the years, it has been evident the color of their skin has played a significant part in their lives.

I have seen opportunities given to other athletes in the athletic arena, not because they possessed the exceptional skills but simply because they portrayed the image the high school desired. Imagine the surprise when my sons were finally put into a position as a last resort, only to have them complete amazing plays, break records, and carry their teams to places their school has not been in decades.

If only they could have looked past their undercover racist tendencies to see the true value of the athletes right in front of them. Martin Luther King, Jr's quote, "The ultimate measure of a man is not where he stands in moments of comfort and convenience, but where he stands at times of challenge and controversy," is tattooed on the chest of my youngest son as a reminder.

I have often told my children that sometimes people would disappoint them with their behavior, that it doesn't mean they needed to stoop to their level and behave poorly too.

Behavior speaks to character. That's what we have to remember. Victory will come quietly when you realize you don't have to prove your worth by making others feel worthless. That is a principle I have tried to raise my children on. The victory will come to you quietly…But should we wait quietly for the victory?

When Trevon Martin was killed by George Zimmerman on February 26, 2012, my oldest son was studying aerospace engineering at the University of Miami. I immediately became scared for him. He wore hoodies. He liked Skittles. He had no reason to fear walking down the street, or at least I didn't think so. That could have been my son who was perceived as a threat simply because he is Black. That could have been my son who was killed. My heart ached for Trevon's parents.

I could not imagine losing my son to such a tragedy. I was angry but I did not use my voice. I did not want it to be about me. I did not want to bring attention to myself because I did not want to act like I knew the heaviness on the shoulders of Black people who have dealt with prejudice and racism their entire lives. These burdens and fears have plagued their families for generations. They earned the right to be angry, I felt I had not. I sat in anger silently. Again.

I have been a nurse for over 20 years. In the healthcare field, we care for many people from different walks of life. We cannot choose *not* to care for a patient who may have killed a grandmother because of his choice to drink and drive. We must provide after-surgery care for an incarcerated patient locked up for molesting a child.

One of the hardest things I have had to do is find empathy for the patient who degraded a nursing assistant because of the color of her skin, so I changed her assignment so she would avoid dealing with such racism.

In retrospect, I had accommodated the request of this patient, seemingly, by condoning his behavior. I had remained silent again. The racist behavior of patients seems to have become more prevalent through the past several years. They are not hiding it. They are not remaining silent. I have come to realize neither should I.

I no longer change assignments unless it is requested by a coworker. I no longer rationalize this behavior as situational. Instead I will tell such a patient that I will not tolerate poor treatment of our staff. In our facility I became an advocate for policy that would include creating a safety plan to help staff dealing with disruptive patients.

The safety plan is now escalated to include administratively discharging a patient if they do not treat our staff with respect and dignity. We are backed by our hospital administrators and our staff feel more protected than they ever have before.

I had a hard time watching the video of the murder of George Floyd on May 25, 2020. As a mother, my heart broke hearing that man call for his own. I was sickened by the lack of compassion for this man by the officers suffocating the life out of him.

As a nurse, I could see signs of his life slowly leaving his body. It is something I still cannot wrap my head around. I recalled a time a few months before I had put myself between a 6'4" aggravated patient, a police officer, and security guard. The patient was Black and I was scared, not for the police officer or the security guard, and certainly, not for myself. I was scared for my patient. I was afraid something would happen to him. I was afraid the officers would interpret any quick movement as threatening. He was intimidating but not to me. I was willing to give him the benefit of the doubt, because too many would not.

He did not need to be feared. He did not need to be slammed to the ground. He needed to be given the respect he deserved. He needed to be listened to, even if he felt he needed to raise his voice to do so.

Not once did he disrespect me throughout this process. De-escalating a situation takes skill. De-escalation can be done without killing someone. I am thankful I was able to be a voice of reason for my patient. He returned to his room without incident and the officers' presence was no longer necessary.

Another time, my daughters and I were on our way to the store when I came across a car crash that happened only a few minutes before. As I pulled over and got out of my car, a bystander called me over to the vehicle that caused the accident. A man in the driver's seat was not responding to any attempts to awaken him. I felt for a pulse…it was there. His breathing was very shallow. I found a hypodermic needle on the floor of his car and it appeared he had overdosed while he was driving. He slammed into the side of an older couple's vehicle but they did not appear to be injured.

What kind of person would I have been if I had chosen to withhold Narcan from him? I maintained his airway and monitored his heart rate and respirations. Then I administered Narcan after his respiratory rate dropped below 8 breaths per minute. He may have committed a crime but he did not deserve to die. It was not my place to be the judge, jury, nor the executioner. George Floyd's murderers had no place either.

Since the COVID-19 pandemic started, I have heard many people end their conversations with "Stay safe out there" but it is not COVID-19 that causes me to give a warning to my sons when they leave the house. I realized for the last several years every time I said goodbye to my sons, I would say "Be safe, please. I love you." Safe, because I am never sure when a traffic stop for a speeding ticket will become deadly for them. I am never sure when a white cop's stereotype of a Black man will cloud their judgement of my son and leave him on the pavement struggling to breathe or bleeding to death.

I used to teach my kids to not see color when they look at other people but that has since changed drastically. We must see color in order to appreciate and respect the lives of people of color. We must see color because we have to see that this does not happen to white people. It is happening to black people at alarmingly high rates.

Open your eyes. See color. See this racism. See that we all need to speak up. Take your blinders off for a moment and see that the system is failing people of color.

Saying "Black Lives Matter" does not lessen the worth of white people. It is about recognizing the worth of people of color so that when you say, "all lives matter," it is true. We all have an obligation to become informed, acknowledge the injustices, and stand with people of color in the fight against racism. Be an advocate for change. Become intolerant of racism. Use your voice.

To remain in silence is to scream in agreement.

I have remained silent for too long.

Shed Your Privilege

By Pamela Brannon

I have spent the better part of my professional career working in nonprofit. I remember a beloved Mr. Rogers' quote from years ago to "look for the helpers," and I never forgot that powerful call to action.

I began volunteering at a local AIDS service organization in Washington, D.C., and joined their buddy program. In those days, most people living with AIDS were shunned and disowned by their families.

I was in college and had no real-world experience but knew deep in my heart I wanted to be a helper -to let someone know their life mattered.

My first buddy was Charles, a gay Black man who lived in Southeast D.C., and I could not have loved him more. He called me "Snowflake," and we became the best of friends.

I took him grocery shopping, out to eat, and to doctor's appointments. He had the biggest crush on Malcolm-Jamal Warner and we joked about planning their wedding. Charles loved to laugh. His laugh lives in my heart to this day. I will never forget the last time I saw him. He was hospitalized, and we knew his time was slipping away. Though he couldn't speak on that last visit, I knew he felt my presence, and I gratefully was given the opportunity to tell him how much I loved him.

When he died, I felt like a member of my own family had died and, in fact, one had. He was like an older brother and I grieved for weeks. He helped me in ways I could have never repaid to him, had he lived long enough to receive life-saving treatments for HIV/AIDS.

The experience with Charles happened 30 years ago and set my feet upon a path of love and service I remain upon to this day.

About 10 years ago, I had a conversation with a donor who supported the organization I manage, Children of Uganda (COU). She is a professor at a university in Kentucky and possessed an infectious spirit. Her deep desire to sponsor one of our children (we serve vulnerable children in Uganda) was palpable. I remember her telling me privilege is invisible when we are discussing the inequalities of our children and how poverty benefits the dominant culture.

For years, I have been enormously blessed to work with Black women, both here and abroad, through COU. They have stood up time and time again to protect our children and make their lives better. They have held my feet to the fire and helped me grow in ways that were often uncomfortable but always deeply constructive.

A few days after George Floyd was murdered, I received two messages from COU graduates who both had U.S. events on their hearts. This is not unusual as I maintain close contact with many of our students, past and present. One of them, a young man named Henry, seemed quite concerned about me. I responded to him with one sentence: "Things are not good in the U.S." His response made me pause. "Because of COVID or racism?" he asked. I responded, "both."

He asked me to be careful and said he would be praying for our nation. Without speaking his name, I knew Henry's life had been impacted by the death of George Floyd.

Our U.S. team is enraged and deeply saddened by the deaths of Ahmad Arbery, Breonna Taylor, and George Floyd, to only name three of the many Black and indigenous men, women, and children who have been killed or injured by law enforcement.

Black Lives Matter.

Our organization has two core values: child safety and child equality in Uganda. The services we provide to all the students in our program are provided through this lens. This commitment must compel us to protect and assist as we do in Uganda.

In this nation, young Black people are three times more likely to be shot by the police than white people. This, coupled with deep inequality in employment, housing, and basic needs tells me it's time for us to take action.

The U.S. team is pledging to do the work necessary to dismantle racial injustice in our own communities. By doing so, we hope to demonstrate to the youth of Uganda that change is possible. We must show that equality and safety is something we practice on both sides of the pond.

These are the actions we pledge to take moving forward:

1. I listened to President Barack Obama speak at a town hall meeting on reimagining policing in our nation. He has asked all of us to reach out to our mayors, city councils, and police oversight bodies to address policies on the use of force by the police. Our U.S. team and board of directors will be doing this in our communities.

2. We are going to seek to recognize our own privilege.

3. We will work with social justice experts to learn and unlearn patterns that cause harm to marginalized communities.

4. We will donate to local and national organizations doing the heavy lifting of anti-racist and anti-oppression work.

Our board of directors is a diverse group of individuals. Their leadership has deeply shaped the culture of COU and redefined how we deliver services.

Some changes have been incremental but they have profoundly improved our ability to be relevant in the lives of the people we serve. Our mission is one that rejects white supremacy and embraces the work of anti-racism. We are committed to breaking the chains of dependency and empowering the beneficiaries in our program with all the skills they need to be self-supporting and thrive. We focus on partnerships! We do not share the historical charity mindset of many organizations; we see our beneficiaries as true partners in creating a better world.

I am also adopting a Black daughter from Uganda. Her name is Vanessa. This has been a two-year process and I am still working with a U.S. based adoption agency and U.S. and Ugandan attorneys to make this long-held dream a reality. My deep desire to become Vanessa's mother comes with the responsibility of learning and unlearning, recognizing my blind spots and doing all I can to mitigate any harm I might cause her as a privileged person-no matter how unintentional.

I have at times questioned myself: who am I, a woman privileged to walk the world clothed in white skin, to direct COU and become a mother of a Black daughter? I am then confronted with my reality. I am a person who feels the pain of the oppressed. I am a person who doesn't close my eyes to injustice. I am a person who is involved in the work of change. I am the executive director of COU and the mother of a beautiful daughter from Uganda, and I wear these titles with deep pride and humility.

When George Floyd was murdered, something deep inside me

shifted. My work team and I have discussed our collective rage and each pledged to do something in this fight, no matter how imperfect. Galvanized by the activists from around the world who have been peacefully protesting and demanding action to stop the violence against Black lives, we know COU's contribution to this cause will not be in vain.

I invite you to join these efforts or pursue the ones you are most called to. Please do not feel you are ill-equipped for this work. If you have a pulse, you have a purpose in this movement.

Stand up when you see inequality. Do not let your privilege be invisible any longer.

Slaying the Goliath of Partiality

By Akeya Carter

If, however, you are [really] fulfilling the law according to the Scripture, "You shall love your neighbor as yourself [that is, if you have unselfish concern for others and do things for their benefit]" you are doing well. But if you show partiality [prejudice, favoritism] you are committing sin and are convicted by the Law as offenders. -James 2:8-9 (AMP)

Justice is defined as "the use of power as appointed by law, honor or standards to support fair treatment and due reward" (Merriam-Webster's Collegiate Dictionary, 2018). Justice is not always fair, nor is it color blind.

People often use their power and privilege to oppress those who differ from themselves in the name of justice. As a Woman of Faith, mother, daughter, and member of Delta Sigma Theta Sorority, Inc. standing on the shoulders of matriarchs, using my influence to fight social injustices comes as naturally as breathing. God blessed me with lanterns to light my path in the form of my mother and grandmothers and become the scholar activist I am today.

My mother and grandmother raised me to believe that I was no better than one person, and that no one person was better than me. As a little girl my mother pushed me to celebrate my Blackness as a source of pride and gift from God in a community where Blackness meant second class, unintelligent, disadvantaged, and dangerous.

When I sat down to write this chapter I prayed. I asked God to give me the courage to be vulnerable and authentic about my first

Goliath. As my granny used to say, "If you are going to pray a dangerous prayer, be prepared to do what God requires."

As a child growing up in southern West Virginia, I unfortunately was exposed to the sin of "partiality," also known as racism, before I lost my first tooth. My thirst for knowledge and inquisitive nature oftentimes has landed me into trouble. Even as I type this, I am shaking thinking about my first encounter with a racist.

As a first grader, I was excited to finally attend the big school. Many of my white classmates were raised to mistrust or stay away from what was different, which in my case meant not to play with the colored girl or the "nigger," as one mother yelled at her son after seeing him play tag with me at recess.

I am 34 years old, so this was the early 90s. I know now hate is a learned behavior. God did not create any of us with racism in mind, and I also know all too well that when sin runs deep, it can be an incredible trial to face.

Here goes… help me Holy Ghost!

At first glance my first-grade teacher seemed pleasant and eager to teach her students. I will call her Mrs. White. She was short with red hair, evergreen eyes, and a bright smile. I soon found out she would become a threat to my education and God-given purpose.

I remember the day she slapped me after calling me a "cheating nigger." That day, something inside of me died, but my mother refused to let me shrink myself. She pushed me to pursue justice and equality regardless of the size of my Goliath, and the David in me was awoken.

From the moment I first entered her classroom, Mrs. White made me into the source of her insecurities and fears. During the first parent teacher conference of the year she tried to bully my mother into placing me in special education. She felt that I was unable to learn on the same level as my peers. Little did she know, my quiet nature was not an indicator of my inability to learn but a defense mechanism to keep from being made fun of by the other children for being too smart.

As the only Black child in the class I was a target from the beginning. I was made of all the same organs and tissues as the white children, but my skin color was the focus. My mother would not hear any of Mrs. White's nonsense. She informed her that I was tested for gifted at my old school but was too young to enter the program.

As school progressed, I noticed Mrs. White never called me by my name. She always referred to me as "girl." One day, as Mrs. White was handing back our spelling tests, I did not get mine back. Most students were happy to place their tests in their take-home folders, so I raised my hand to ask where mine was. Mrs. White looked at me disgusted and yelled, "Cheaters go to the principal's office!"

With tear-filled eyes, I walked down the hall toward the principal's office. My granny and I had practiced all week on my spelling list. I knew I had not cheated. Ms. Coleman, the school principal, was a pleasant woman. She explained to me that she had to call my mother since cheating accusations were very serious. While I waited in the office for my mother to arrive, I wondered what I had done to be treated so badly by my teacher. My mother arrived and Ms. Coleman spoke with her before calling Mrs. White to the office.

After she arrived, my mother suggested I retake my test in front of them and Ms. Coleman agreed. Of course, Mrs. White protested but Ms. Coleman immediately dismissed her argument. My mother reached into her purse and pulled out the tablet she often let me doodle on during church services. Ms. Coleman asked my mother and Mrs. White to wait in the lobby while she retested me.

Just like my original test paper I spelled every word correctly, including a new bonus word from Ms. Coleman. She called my mother and Mrs. White back to her office. Mrs. White seemed even more agitated that I had passed the test but with the matter settled Ms. Coleman sent me back to class with Mrs. White. On the way back to class, Mrs. White grabbed my arm, squeezing until I began to cry, and said "girl, you need to learn your place, you're nothing but a cheating nigger!"

Her slap burned like my finger after accidentally touching a stove. I felt helpless and scared. Ms. Hunter, a second-grade teacher saw the entire incident. I thank God for her because I am not sure how far things would have gone that day or if anyone would have believed me. In that moment, every aspiration and dream I had died. Mrs. White had won, or so I thought, as I began to believe the things she said about me.

Ms. Hunter immediately took me into her arms and rubbed my back asking me to go sit in her classroom. Soon after I heard a sound coming from the principal's office. I am not sure what my mother said or did but Mrs. White ran faster than anyone I have ever seen in my life.

For the first time, I felt as if God himself could not even protect me. I had been raised to be unapologetically Black and brilliant, in that moment I prayed for Him To make me white.

I wasn't quite sure how prayer worked. All I knew was what I had been taught in Sunday School; that whatever we asked of the Father in the name of Jesus would be granted.

My prayer was to become white as cotton. For the rest of the day, I sat in my room as my mother and grandmother met with the NAACP and church leadership. I cried until my head hurt but I never stopped praying to become white. I remember pleading with God through my tears. *Please, God make me white and pretty like all the other kids.*

Mrs. White was transferred to another school. The Superintendent of Schools issued a written apology to me and my mother. For many years, I never looked at school quite the same. How could Mrs. White still be able to teach children after the way she treated me?

I also questioned why God had still not answered my only prayer. One evening at dinner, I told my granny I hated my teacher and school. She lovingly smiled at me saying "Keya there is no room for hate in a child of God's heart. Your teacher was wrong but God can soften even her hateful heart, pray God unhardened her heart."

Many years would go by before I found the strength to forgive her but once I did, I realized the problem had been her inability to look past my skin color. She hated what I represented: change in the "equal not equitable" educational system. My potential and gifts were the issue since she feared what she could not understand or control.

Today, the incident that nearly destroyed me fuels my quest to teach my students about the sin of partiality, or racism. Each semester I teach my students that it is not the presence of Black people that activates social injustices but the presence of ambition and intelligence combined with ignorance and excuses.

Standing against social injustices requires risk and preparation. I view those who commit injustices as opponents on the battlefield of life. At six years old God knew the plans He had for me, and so did the enemy.

My David experience with Mrs. White charted the course I am on today. I do not do my work for fame or credit but because from the moment God began forming me in my mother's womb, Mrs. White was a part of the plan for my life.

I have faced many Mrs. Whites throughout my life, each time reminded that I was created in the likeness and image of God. So, if someone opposes me because I am Black, a woman, or even short, then they stand in direct opposition of the God who created me.

Much like David, I did not ask to wear the armor of a social activist, but I am honored to wear it on the battlefield of equality daily.

1 Samuel 16:7 (NIV) says:

> *The LORD does not look at the things people look at.*
> *People look at the outward appearance, but the*
> *LORD looks at the heart.*

As a scholar-activist, I use intellectual theory to empower and train others to look at the heart of racism and social injustices. Seeing social injustice through God's eyes has helped me appeal to the mind, will, and emotions of my opponents. I want to encourage others to take up their social justice sling shots and smooth stones to slay the racist, prejudice, and oppressive Goliaths who pose a threat to the kingdom of God and his creation.

Together We Can

By Kimberly Caylor-White

*Sometimes rather than climb that mountain, we strap it on our back and try to carry it. We become broken, and in even more pain, before we finally realize that climbing it is the only way…*Teresa L Holmes

To those of you whom I may offend, I apologize. My beliefs will remain the same and I will continue to speak their truths.

I am a Christian. I believe in love and worship my God and Jesus. I believe each and every word in the Bible, but unfortunately there are people throughout history who have twisted those words, such as the people who believed that slavery was acceptable, that people should have relationships only within their own race, and that white people are superior. To those people: you need a refresher course in understanding your Bible.

The Bible states in Revelations that Jesus was of bronze color with wooly hair, which is a far cry from the pictures that depict him as white with long, straight, brown hair. The killing of Jesus by the Romans could even be thought of as the beginning of "white washing," whether done intentionally or accidentally. It is hard to pray to and worship someone your own people chose to kill.

It is common for people to "white-wash" the history of people of color, as people with darker skin have historically been displaced, diseased, enslaved, and killed. This seeing of the world with rose colored glasses happens because people are ashamed of their actions or that their own ancestors could have also been of a darker complexion.

Plainly stated, if Jesus is Black, that means every human being has at least 1 drop of that darker color running through their veins. We are all simply different shades of the same color!!

Find, accept, and embrace that truth. It should not be disregarded. It is our history.

This racism has existed throughout history, dating back centuries and still existing today. It is the unadulterated hatred of another person simply due to their skin color. Throughout history, democracy, freedom, opportunity and prosperity have been mostly reserved for everyone but people of color, as they are denied access to fair housing, quality education, healthcare, jobs, and equal justice.

Change must be across the board to ensure that people of color are given the same opportunities as everyone else in America. Accountability must be across the board to protect all communities from racism and social injustice. Each young man, woman, and child needs to believe that their life matters and that they must fight for all people of color.

On March 14, 2013, Wayne Jones, a black man, was shot 22 times by four white police officers. Mr. Jones was a homeless man who had been diagnosed with schizophrenia. Unable to comprehend their request, Wayne Jones was shot down while walking in the middle of the street in downtown Martinsburg, West Virginia.

The coroner ruled Mr. Jones' death a homicide, but the Grand Jury refused to indict. On July 21st, 2020, his family was awarded 3.5

million dollars in damages after it was ruled that Mr. Jones was both secured and incapacitated in the final moments of his life. The family hired a new attorney to once again pursue charges against the officers involved in this tragic situation.

The death of George Floyd has shaken this country. I, as so many others, watched Mr. Floyd plead for his life. We heard him repeatedly say he could not breathe, heard him call out for his mother, and watched as he took his final breath. We also as bystanders' pleas were ignored and as four other officers refused to intervene. This was cold blooded murder. I am heartbroken. I feel helpless, guilty, and angry.

I am ashamed of our United States President for not speaking out and bringing peace to the nation. I am angry at his blatantly racist ideology and the way he condones the actions of hate by his supporters. I am also angry at every politician who has not had the courage to put a stop to this behavior.

Racism did not start with President Trump, and it will not end with him, but he has surely exploited it for his own agenda.

Are racists a product of their environment? Personally, I think not. They may have been born into it and raised by a racist family. They may have become friends with a racist. As people grow, becoming older and wiser, they are responsible for their own thoughts and actions. They have the ability to break the cycle and change the course of their life and community.

Racist behavior exists due to biases and practices designed to oppress people of color, and white people benefit from these. White privilege does not mean authority over others, is not a license to hurt others, and does not give anyone the right to take a life.

White privilege means that being white, a person has never been disliked and hated for the color of their skin. Their lives may be difficult due to other factors, but they have never been judged for their skin tone as people of color have for centuries.

Racists live in fear as well. They are threatened by what they do not know and what they do not understand. Being American is not divided by race, color, gender, or sexual orientation. Being American means being divided into the wise and the fools.

Fools are the people who divide themselves by race, color, gender, sexual orientation, and stupidity.

I fear for my children and family every day. I fear for my son. I fear for my husband and his family. I fear turning on the tv and hearing that another life, the life of a person of color, has once again been unjustly taken, especially by the people sworn to protect us. I fear that people may become immune, desensitized to these senseless acts of hate.

To fight racism we need a system, a strategy. We need solidarity, freedom, and to forgive. If there is hate in our hearts, true change cannot happen. We must listen and hear each other. That is how change happens. We must hear the pain of others. We must empathize and care. We must demand change.

This country must be held accountable for its participation in reinforcing injustice. Resolution cannot happen without confrontation. We cannot be complicit or get comfortable in this fight. Listen to people of color and hear their pain. They are more than their skin color and agonizing past.

Men of color – stand up! We need your strength. We need your leadership.

Women of color – continue to raise your children with love, respect, humility, and discipline.

Children and young adults of color – you are the future! We desperately need you! Grow with an enthusiasm to learn, see change in your community and fight for those changes.

Most importantly for all – never let your fire burn out. Light up this world with love, unity, and equal justice for all.

As Representative John Lewis once said: Democracy is not a state. It is an act...

Together we can heal the soul of America.

Experiencing Racism

By Angela Coley

I spent birth until age 16 as an Army brat. My family traveled to different places in the world. During that time, I attended five different elementary schools, two different junior high schools, and a high school. None of these school systems provided transportation, so we walked.

Throughout my travels, I met people of all races but to me everyone was the same. Many of them were my friends. We had birthday parties together, sleepovers, went to the movies, and played outside every day and night.

In 1983, the nightmare began for me. My dad retired from the Army and moved my family to Georgia, where he had roots.

My mom and grandmother were from England. There were eight in our family: my dad, mom, grandmother, three sisters, my brother, and myself. We started out living with my aunt and her family in a small, three-bedroom, one-bath, older home. My aunt was a bus driver, and for the first time ever I rode the bus to school.

We were 11 people, crammed into one small home, all trying to perform daily activities and get to wherever we were going. Things began to get difficult. After school, I couldn't find a seat on the bus. No one wanted to sit with me. Then the name calling started. "Half Breed" and "Oreo" were a few of the terms that were used but it got worse. While sitting in class trying to hold a conversation with a Caucasian girl, I noticed that she was ignoring me. Then, a boy intervened.

"Only *we* sit over here."

"Who is *we*?" I thought.

Then the boy pointed it out for me. There was a white and a Black side in the classroom. Never had I experienced this. Being divided by race was foreign to me.

It was the same during recess. Caucasians hung out on one side of the hall while the African Americans hung out on the other. I had no clue why this was happening. In any other place I had lived everyone was considered equal.

I thought it could not get any worse but I was wrong. We moved from my aunt's house to live with my great-grandmother. She lived in an old singlewide, one-bedroom mobile home with no bathroom or running water. We had to sleep on the floor, sometimes using kitchenware as a toilet and carrying empty jugs down a dirt road to our neighbor's house to get water. Nothing like this ever happened when my dad was in the army.

During summer vacation, my dad found a three-bedroom house with a convenience store and gas station connected that he was interested in buying. The house was situated in Allentown, Georgia, a place so small everyone knew each other. The house was owned by a well-known Caucasian who was now deceased, and the local bank was hesitant to sell to an African American man. Finally, my mom and my grandmother, who were of another race, went to the bank and were approved for the house with no problem, even though they were both unemployed.

When the people in Allentown realized my dad was married to the lady that bought the house, the tension began. Still he was determined to not be deterred. We were all so happy to finally have a house of our own.

My dad still had to fight to open the store and the gas station though. The local city hall kept giving him a difficult time. That was another fight my dad did with such determination. Finally, his paperwork was approved.

Why were they trying so hard to keep an African American down? Did he not have the right to operate a business just like any other human? Why treat him differently because of the color of his skin?

After much struggle, my dad opened his own business, Whipple's Grocery Store. He wanted to sell alcohol but that was denied. He then tried for a game room and received further push back. Finally, he decided to take things into his own hands and without permission purchased a pool-table and three arcade machines. It was only African Americans who frequented the store anyway. Why not take that chance?

With so much happening, the summer seemed to go by quickly. Soon it was back to school time. I started hanging with the wrong crowd, trying to fit in somewhere but ending up failing ninth grade. I tried summer school but that did not help. After buckling down and focusing, I passed to the tenth grade and started a job at Dairy Queen in Dublin, Georgia.

While working there, a customer, who was Caucasian, showed up often just to chat with me. He wanted to drive me home and after continuously insisting, I finally accepted.

It did not take long for my manager to figure out what was going on. She was also Caucasian and did not believe in mixed races dating. Whenever my guy-friend was in the parking lot waiting for me to get off work, my manager would make him leave. He would go until it was time for me to get off work and then return.

Our relationship did not last long. The pressure from work and school became too much. It seemed that we were fighting with so many others just to be together, and it took its toll.

Even though I hoped it would be different by now, racism is still running rampant. My most recent personal encounter was while working for the U.S. Federal Government. I had free hotel stays with the casinos and invited a Caucasian co-worker to join me at no cost if she would drive her car.

One night, she started drinking alcohol. After exceeding her limit, she became quite talkative. It is said that the only people who will tell you the truth are a drunk and a child, and her truth was certainly revealed. She brought up my accomplishments at work, and I asked her why.

She stated, "**You people** are always doing something, thinking you are better than everyone else." She then went on and on, expressing her true feelings about African Americans.

I was so shocked and speechless. I cried myself to sleep that night. The next morning, she repeatedly apologized. I did not say a word,

I just wanted to go home. If I had driven my car, I would have left her at the casino.

The entire drive back home I kept thinking about everything she and I used to do together. I could pick up no signs of racism.

Going back to work and being around her was difficult, I had no conversation for her. Finally, I applied and was accepted for a job in another department.

After all that has happened to my family and me that was related to race, I still see no color. I believe we were all created equal and I will not let the actions of others sway me from that belief. We all bleed the same and for equality, I will stand even when others stand against me.

Racism: Don't Let it Break You, Let Faith Make You

By Rebecca Davis

The world will try to break you. That is what it is like for a person of color who happens to be "mixed." I stand, boots on the ground, for all Black people regardless of hue, shape, hair texture, or percentage of blackness. Racism and colorism from within and out must stop.

My mothers are angels on Earth. My biological mom hid her pregnancy from her parents for about six months to prevent termination. The only way something like that is possible is God. When they discovered her pregnancy, they sent her to a home for unwed mothers. My mother also "forgot" to mention to her parents that I am Black. What a surprise when they saw my brown skin!

While one white family had refused to keep me, another white family accepted me with open arms and love. My adoptive family had already adopted two boys, one white like them and one brown like me. My mother endured terrible comments in the stores. She is an angel for loving us all unconditionally with the love of a mom who had birthed her own children. One way she helped us to fit into the family was to tell us how beautiful our brown skin and dark curls were. True love, after all, is not affected by color.

As an adult, this beautiful story can make me feel guilty. I have experienced my share of racism. At times, I was protected because of my family. My experiences were not that of my peers. My dad was a doctor, which came with some privilege. Compared to my peers, I had opportunities that some didn't. We traveled and took some vacations. Privilege. My parents both went to college and had degrees. Privilege. I had resources available that others didn't. They didn't spoil me with material things. I had everything I needed and a little more.

When I played sports, I didn't have to worry about equipment, proper shoes, transportation, or if someone would be in the stands for me. At least one, if not both of my parents, would be there. Privilege. I was 10 when I first started to see differences in how I was treated. I imagine my peers saw racism up close and personal much sooner. Privilege.

It was about this same time that I wanted to be a cheerleader. I knew all the cheers, so the coach was sure I'd make the team. For tryouts, I was put on the end of the line. The woman selecting the squad looked at me only once. Needless-to-say, I didn't make it. I was overlooked but not because I wasn't good enough. The Fayetteville Browns cheerleaders apparently couldn't be brown.

It was when I left that small town that a surprising discrimination started. We moved in town during my teen years and some of the worst discrimination against me would occur from people who looked like me. While I did not fit into the white community for obvious reasons, I didn't fit into the black community either. Why was the color of my skin labeled as white girl, zebra, or yellow? How did I speak "too white?" Who determines if someone's hair is "good" or not? What makes hair that is not 4C a reason to discriminate?

There was nothing I could do to change the shade of my skin, my hair texture, the parents who raised me, the shape of my nose, and the plumpness of my lips or backside. I wondered if I would ever fit in because of who I am and not what I looked or sounded like.

I realized that maybe I was not meant to fit in, I was meant to stand out. I was meant to break barriers and help create change. In the end, I have the best friends of all races. I didn't let the treatment from any race keep me down. I will never let the critical eye of others keep me from flourishing and being who God created me to be.

When I was in school, I didn't have the trouble that some of my friends had. I got good grades, I was athletic, and I stayed out of trouble. Some of my friends graduated illiterate. They were needed to play sports and to win the game, so some of the teachers kept passing them on to the next level whether they should have moved up a grade or not. This set them up for failure. They were deemed good enough to play the game but not given the skills necessary to succeed in life.

My mom and I were plagued with guilt when awards and scholarships were given out for the minority students my senior year of high school. I received awards to go to college for my academics that I didn't need and could have been used by someone else. My family had the money for college.

Some of my friends didn't make it into college. We attended the same high school, but they didn't get the same education. These students could have accomplished more if only there had been a level playing field. If the students mattered for who they were and not the ball they carried, their education could have carried them farther. If their education mattered, they could have been set for future careers rather than being siphoned into the jail system.

I have seen firsthand how minority students, especially those with special needs, are filtered out of the regular school system instead of finding what will help them graduate from the regular schools.

All children are our future. We can't afford to leave any behind. College should always be an option. Providing opportunity is not lowering the bar, it is setting the stage for everyone to succeed. If one lane is given a head start and the other lanes of the track have an obstacle course, the finish line is only readily attainable to that one lane. If the track is equal in length with the same number, height and spacing of the hurdles, the finish line is attainable to all.

It is more important now than ever that schools be filled with teachers of all ethnicities. I didn't see my first Black teacher until I was 11 or 12. It is important that young students see adults who look like them in places of authority, not just in places of service. The disparities are evident. I may never have seen myself as a teacher if I had not had Mrs. Jiles in seventh grade.

There is more to life than what kids see out the window, in the street, at the playground, on the music video, in the movie or even sometimes in their own homes. President Barack Obama was more than a President; he was an icon for all students to see that we have overcome. People of color can be and do anything.

As parents, we need to challenge our children without expecting others to fill in the gaps. Not all teachers will take the time to make sure that your student is properly prepared. The risk is too great.

The color of our skin is unfairly seen as a weapon. An arsenal of a strong mind and strong vocabulary are the weapons we need to be armed with. Degrees, diplomas, an education, and a growth mindset cannot be taken away. We must be armed and dangerous with the power of an education. Whether it be formal education or learning a trade from YouTube, the power of the mind is a terrible thing to waste.

As a teacher, I have witnessed and even fallen into suppressing our Black young ladies. Our dominant future female leaders of America who happen to be Black are often told that they are too loud. When I was mentoring these young women, I'd explain to them how they are perceived to be.

I will always mentor but I will not tell them to tone it down any longer. I realize that it is not the loudness of the voice that is the problem, it is the leadership qualities that these young women possess that are perceived as threatening. Had I forgotten that I was loud as a child and teenager, too? My dream occupations were those of a leader.

We need to be mindful of who and what we are suppressing. We could be crushing our youths' dreams by constantly squashing who they are and who they were born to be. We need to embrace the qualities of our children and encourage them to develop skills that match who they are meant to be.

In my class, I like to teach the poem "Dreams" by Langston Hughes. "Hold fast to dreams."

If you were denied your dream as a child, embrace it. Pick it up now and be who people said you couldn't be.

My family has always been a little mixed up. We had stares from the time we were babies till now. When my little one, whose father is white, was born with skin lighter than mine and straight, brown hair, I was afraid that someone would think I took her.

This may sound funny. However, a Caucasian family with Black children is sort of normal these days. But a Caucasian looking baby with a Black family? I wouldn't risk it. She looks like me, but she doesn't look Black at all. I carried proof just in case. Now that she is older, I don't carry it anymore because she can speak for herself.

As a parent of Black children, we are forced to do things differently. My parents didn't teach us how to be pulled over and live to tell about it or how to visit a friend's house. Since my parents were both white, I was raised white. They didn't have the experiences, so they didn't know any differently. After all, we were their children. They loved and raised us as their own.

Education and conversation are two of the greatest things that we can have to make race relations better. Reform has to happen to inspire equality in all areas. Right now, people from all over the world are recognizing the plight for what it is and are joining in the fight to make change happen. I have friends of all races standing with me, with their boots on the ground, to make change. Some are on the frontlines at rallies making sure people know why change needs to happen for everyone.

As parents, we teach our children how to do many things. One thing we must focus on is love. We must teach children how to love themselves for who they are and to love others the same. My mom taught me my skin and hair are beautiful. I didn't question it until my teen years of not being white or not quite black enough.

Colorism still happens today. People have made comments about my "white side." I don't have a side. I am me. Because of my one drop, I am Black.

I pray for people who put others down. I pray that those who are racist will embrace these times of change. Together, we can be the example to change the minds of the world.

All of my life experiences have only made me stronger. I have relied on God to get me through everything. Life was not always easy, but through faith in Him I was able to survive. It has become my mission to make a positive impact and help other women and teens make their lives the best they can.

I developed the Rebekah Project 3:19, my ministry, to send positive messages into the world. I was inspired to write a book called "Living Your Life and Loving Those in It." It is a scripture-based book that deals with forgiving and loving yourself and others to live your best life.

We need to use God's word to sweeten up our lives. One way we can sprinkle sugar on this life full of lemons is to love everyone. Love conquers a multitude of sin. We need to first sprinkle a little sugar of love on ourselves and then love others. There is strength in forgiveness and releasing yourself from the hurt and pain.

My Black is beautiful, your Black is beautiful. Your shade of skin is beautiful.

We are better together.

Thirsting for Justice

By Layne Diehl

Aubrey Lane White was a United States Navy World War II veteran. He was my uncle and I am his namesake. My maternal grandfather, Glenn Everett Robinson, was an engineer for the United States Army on a railroad in India during the same time. My father, Ervin Lacy Windon, was a Vietnam veteran. Born into a family of American pride, I was either inherently blessed with a strong sense of justice or developed it quickly through my raising.

I spent my formative years in Fort Worth, Texas, and remember the little boy at summer camp who was unfairly declined a piece of candy while all the other children were joyfully given one. I remember the young Black child in my third-grade private school class who cried as he was taunted for the color of his skin. I remember the confusion of living in a racist south where integration was strongly resisted, and children were bussed to the other side of town for one year of their secondary education to study alongside those of different ethnic origins.

At the time I was young and not able to fully understand the significance of these events. I could feel the need for justice rising in me even then, though I would learn as I matured that my opinions and perceptions of what justice was were largely colored by the systemic racism of our time.

Law and government were intriguing subjects to me in school. I believed that equality and liberty were available to all men and women, especially in the United States. As a child and even sometimes as a young adult, when someone did not see my country in the same way that I did, with the same level of pride and gratitude, I felt hurt and offended. These feelings too would evolve in time.

Just as I was about to turn twelve years old, my family went through a dramatic change as my father was transferred to an Air Force base in Arizona. Our family unit did not survive the move and after several months, my brother, mother, and I were on our way back to my parents' hometown in West Virginia to start our lives over. The next several years were hard for my mom, who struggled to raise two kids on her own, with less than half the income we once had. Little did I know that the small town I loved to visit as a child was filled with secrets I wouldn't uncover for years. Small town life was nothing like I imagined, and my family name and the legacy left by those who shared it defined me in ways I didn't fully appreciate until after my father died when I was in my forties.

I learned after I was an adult that when my father was four years old, he witnessed his father's shooting during a domestic violence incident. This happened in that same small town I moved to as a teen. The day after my grandfather was shot and killed, the local paper all but reported that he had it coming. Dad and his siblings endured school and judgment from their peers and the community that day, and for years to come.

My father died with the demons of that trauma. My children and I were estranged from him in the last years of his life because those demons became so dangerous. My family name affected my friendships and my experiences many times without my full comprehension, except possibly in hindsight. It is an unfortunate consequence of living in small town America leaving scars that often take generations to heal.

I recognize that I will never be able to fully empathize with my Black brothers and sisters in the United States. White privilege has benefited me even when my circumstances seemed grim, yet something about being judged because of my family's circumstances and past, something that was completely out of my control, allowed me to experience personal injustice in a way that I had not experienced before the move.

I found myself defined by others and judged by unfair prejudices. We did not have the nice things we once had. We did not live in the white suburban neighborhood that we once did. I was limited in clothes and belongings for the first time in my life. I was treated by many like an outcast. I felt as though I could not escape and was destined for poverty. I rebelled and began a journey down a dark path for several years before I found the light again.

I met my husband Nic in my senior year of high school. For the first time in a long time, I felt kindness and compassion. He was fun and did not judge me. He introduced me to his family and offered me the happiness I had longed for. Had I not met him, I would never have gone to college, as I'd abandoned that notion in high school when a counselor convinced me that I couldn't afford it.

Nic introduced me to a financial aid adviser at Concord College, a local liberal arts school, and helped me to get enrolled. Once the opportunity of higher education was available to me, I regained hope. I studied nonstop. I loved my classes and my professors. I secretly wanted to go to law school.

Aside from my husband, I only told my academic advisor, Dr. Ron Burgher, of my aspirations. Dr. Burgher assisted me in finding a curriculum that would prepare me for law school. He encouraged me and guided me through the admissions process. He wrote a letter of recommendation for me. He found a work study job and congressional internship for me and mentored me.

Dr. Burgher was the first person to open my eyes to the fact that not all people see the world through the same lens. He helped me to understand how life circumstances, trauma, and personal experiences could dramatically shape your outlook on life. He helped me to develop the ability to make a paradigm shift, to see the world as another person may see it, and to attempt empathy.

As part of my work study job at Concord College, I assisted Dr. Burgher in putting together an annual artist lecture series. Speakers during my time there included Sarah Weddington, lead counsel for Jane Roe in the famous United States Supreme Court case of Roe v Wade, and William Kunstler, a National Lawyers Guild attorney who took the Chicago Eight case to Seventh Circuit in the case of the United States v. Dellinger. Both of these speakers and the experience of having them at Concord shaped me. They gave me a perspective in my law practice that I still hold dear today.

When Sarah Weddington came to town, I was not prepared. Opinion leaders on all sides of the debate launched down on the little college in Athens like nothing I'd seen before. Protests and debate broke out on all corners of campus. Tiny plastic fetuses were handed out to students and those in attendance. As someone who had strong opinions about the value of life, I proudly wore a pin made into a tiny pair of bare feet on my lapel. Yet, as the greater conversation on campus began to take shape and arguments were exchanged, I became able to see the other side. A stately but unassuming woman took the stage and with a steady even-tempered voice began to discuss the rationale behind her decision to take the case.

I started to understand that the issue was not one as simple as I'd once thought. Poverty, disease, rape, incest, and other nefarious issues could not be fairly left out of the discussion. The health and care for a woman's own body during what often constituted desperate circumstances could not go unprotected. I began to realize that I could take a position on an issue as it might affect me while respecting the need for a legal system that protected the rights of those less fortunate.

William Kunstler's visit was another fascinating experience. After his speech, he was invited to speak to a small class of Dr. Burgher's students. Just as the class was about to start, the door flung open and the program secretary rushed in to evacuate it. There had been a bomb threat.

Kunstler shrugged as if it was a familiar experience. He looked at the class, his spectacles perched on top of his head, and suggested we find a nice green tree on the lawn outside and continue the discussion. That we did.

He shared with us about the Democratic National Convention in 1968 and the protestors who were arrested and tried. Those arrested and put on trial came to be known as the Chicago Eight. He shared with us about the trial experience, the judge's contempt toward those who had peacefully dissented at the convention, and the public spectacle that ensued. He shared with us about Bobby Seale, a young black protestor who demanded to represent himself. The judge denied his request but as Seale persisted, he was ultimately bound, gagged, and separated from his peers during the trial by a judge who was both cavalier and antagonistic of Seale's constitutional rights.

The Seventh Circuit overturned the case on appeal and reprimanded the judge for his high handedness during the trial. The US Supreme Court denied certiorari on appeal to the high court, allowing the Seventh Circuit's admonishment to stand. In recognition of Seale's being unlawfully denied due process and his fair day in court, Chicago Eight would then be referred to as Chicago Seven.

My years in law school began a new personal challenge for me. I became pregnant, lost a baby, and gave birth to another within the first year. A highly stressful personal experience plagued our new small family making it difficult to concentrate on my studies. The last year of law school, Nic moved to a town an hour and a half away for employment, while my daughter stayed with me to complete my last year of class. Nevertheless, we made it through.

Studying for the bar exam became my next challenge. After months of study and commuting back and forth between the law school in

Morgantown, West Virginia, and Elkins, West Virginia, where Nic was living, I reported to Charleston for the bar.

For the first time in my life, panic struck me as I stared at the exam. Never had I experienced test anxiety yet in the next half hour to an hour, I could not focus on the words on the test. All I could think of was my daughter. I was struck with fear thinking that the only thing standing between her long-term well-being and livelihood was my success on this exam. When I was finally able to get my head together, I had lost critical time. When I got my results, I had missed the mark by less than one point. I was devastated.

More determined than ever and angry with myself, I began to study again the way I'd studied while I was at Concord. Additionally, I found myself a piece of classical piano music and practiced it periodically when I would need a break from studying. I had read that listening to classical music helped students do better on exams so I decided to take it to the next level and learn this classical piece as I studied to take the bar for the second time.

I prepared notecards, outlines, and materials to assist myself in preparation. As I made the journey to Charleston for the second time, Mozart played in the background as I recalled legal concepts one by one. This time I passed with flying colors. I learned in that experience to never let fear get in the way of my progress.

I was given a Bible by the small church we were attending in Elkins as a gift for my law school graduation. The day I was sworn into the bar, I opened that Bible to find the following verse:

Speak up for those who cannot speak for themselves, for the rights of all who are destitute. Speak up and judge fairly; defend the rights of the poor and needy. -Proverbs 31:8-9 (NIV)

A fire stirred in me as the words seemed to jump off the page. It was my life calling. With everything I do in my practice and profession, I try to remember these words. Who are those who can't speak for themselves? How can I use my voice to make the world better for those less fortunate?

As I write this, I have recently, along with the rest of the country, witnessed the horrific video of Jacob Blake of Wisconsin being shot in the back seven times by a law enforcement officer while Blake's three children watched inside of his vehicle. That officer gave no thought to those babies in that car. And those who try to say that Jacob Blake had it coming are not only terribly wrong but have no mercy or grace for the innocence of the children who witnessed it. Those kids have a long road ahead of them and, like my family, will likely suffer for generations as they try to overcome the trauma.

It is the year 2020 and we are now three and a half years into an administration that has shaken our nation's foundation to its core. We have an anger problem in this country. We have a problem with unnecessary force. We have a problem with fear. We have a problem with hate. It was all there before 2016 but Donald Trump has brought to the surface how very deep these problems continue to be. Our brooding racism and cowboy complex have not served us well. We swing our swords around and brandish our weapons with a sense of arrogant pride. We rewrite our history to deny our grievous shortcomings. COVID-19 has now brought us to our knees and maybe there is a reason for that.

I reflect upon my own practice and recognize more clearly how many of my successes and benefits come from standing on the shoulders of black men and women in our country. So many of my colleagues, family, and friends have become emboldened by the current occupant of the White House to speak freely of their racially motivated thoughts and beliefs.

My life may not have always been easy, but my race alone in white America has not been a factor to hold me back and oftentimes gained me an advantage. I've learned that not only do I have family of noble service, but also those who fought alongside their Confederate peers in an effort to preserve slavery. I reflect on moments that my thoughts were not pure from an equality standpoint. I recognize those conversations I may have overheard in boardrooms and back offices that, even if I didn't engage, I failed to speak out against the discriminatory dialogue.

For these reasons, today I seek in addition to justice, an atonement for my part in racial inequality. Atonement for the privilege I have that others don't. Atonement for the slights I have made. Atonement for my ancestors and my country.

God bless every person who has felt bondage and fear in these United States. May He show us a better way to live. May our eyes be open and our hearts receptive. May we all turn to our higher callings so that our better angels can emerge.

I pray for humility and the humbleness that comes from the realization of my own contributions to racism in the United States. Let us realize that until we know the peace that comes through unconditional love, we will never recover. We will be a nation of perpetual civil war with each other. I admit I am weary. I don't want war anymore, not for me nor my children nor for any of the children of this country. Yet, it is only though atonement and a challenge to our current system that the ideals envisioned in our nation's founding can be truly realized, that being equal justice for all in those inalienable rights of life, liberty, and the pursuit of happiness.

This is why I stand.

Prayer Changes Things

By Renee Ferguson

You are not smart enough to be in this group. We cannot play with you because you are Black. I have the right to call you a N-----!

What do you think when you read this? If you are a minority, how do you feel? How do you push past statements like this? If you are not part of the majority, how do you defend yourself? What tools are at your bidding?

Unfortunately, I have heard all these statements directed towards me and my children, and the individuals who spoke them were confident and serious in their delivery. A major portion of my life has been spent learning to properly respond to them verbally, identifying what actions are appropriate to take, and discovering who alongside me would help fight these battles.

At a very young age, a teacher decided to remove me from a higher-level academic group because she said I was not smart enough. I vividly recall her looking me straight in the eyes and saying, "you are not smart enough to be in this group."

Despite my youth, I thought it strange, because other students in the group often sought me out to help with their homework. I politely questioned my teacher, but was told that I would remain in the lower academic group. When I got home, I told my parents, and the next day a meeting was set up between them and my teacher. I was immediately restored to my original group.

You never know the extent people will go when they have hatred in their heart toward another person. My interactions with that teacher did not end with my parents' involvement. The two friends I had at that time were instructed by her not to play with me on the playground because I was Black. Little kids are always open and honest, so my friends came up to me and said, "We cannot play with you because you are Black."

It is funny how my mind worked back then. My solution to my teary-eyed friends was to walk around the playground together at recess; that way, we were not really playing. Fortunately for me, they went home and told their parents, who did not feel the same way as the teacher. Upon their return to school, I was excited to learn they were "allowed" to play with me. This experience at such an early age was just the beginning of what was to come.

I went on to experience similar racial injustices throughout middle school and high school. In high school, my guidance counselor refused to sign my papers for admission to the Naval Academy because he thought that a white boy was more deserving.

Even with all the injustices directed toward me, nothing compared to the feelings I had as a mother when the racial injustices were posed against my children. I remember them all in great detail.

Spring was quickly approaching, and track season had just begun. One of my sons was a middle-distance runner and everyone was excited about how well he was doing for his age. His coach even brought him to practice with the high school team for better competition.

My son loved running and he enjoyed competing against the older kids. At this time, he was unaware that there would be such animosity regarding his recognition.

One day after practice, my son was talking with some of his classmates in the locker room, when one of the boys on the high school team, who he had only met the day before, began tussling with him. He picked my son up from behind and unexpectedly slammed him on the hard locker room floor. My son landed on his head and sustained a very bad concussion, to the extent that he blacked out.

I was waiting to pick him up outside of the school track when I was notified by my son's teammates that he had been hurt. They were in complete disarray and quick to tell me that the incident was completely unprovoked. Like any mother would, I rushed to check on the welfare of my son. By the time I got to the locker room, he was slowly walking out the door. A flood of emotions engulfed me as I heard my son state that his vision was blurry, and his head was hurting.

I could plainly see the bruises on his face. All I wanted to know was who did this, and why. No one seemed to have an explanation. At that point I became furious. I found the coaches and told them what happened to my son. I requested ice from them so that I could place it on my son's bruises. No response. I repeatedly asked for ice. Still no response. My son's teammates who witnessed the incident explained to the coach what happened, in my son's defense, but still nothing was done.

I quickly realized that the coaches were not concerned about my son. It did not matter that he had a concussion, or that he required first aid. A serious assault against an innocent young Black male had just taken place and the high school coaches thought nothing of it. This situation—this denial of justice—was going to be dealt with but first I had to seek medical care for my son.

As I sat in the emergency room at the hospital and waited for my son to be seen by the doctor, all I could think about was how to proceed. God only knows what I wanted to do, but I knew I had to keep my composure. We explained what happened to the emergency room doctor. Once my son's testing was completed, the doctor looked at me and said, "This should not be happening with what is going on right now at Virginia Tech!" A mass shooting had just taken place there. The doctor was angry and said he was going to write the incident up as an assault in his report.

The next day, I went to the high school to see what the administrators there had done to the boy who assaulted my son. To my surprise, there was nothing done nor was there anything planned. The boy was in his regular class and his parents had not been notified of the incident. If it had been my son on the other side of the fence, he would have been suspended. The boy's mother contacted me a few days later. She still had not been told what happened.

There were so many things I wanted to say. So many things I wanted to do. I was an extremely angry mother. I knew deep down inside there was a proper and spiritual way to handle the situation but I would not be telling the truth if I did not admit there was a part of me that wanted to handle the situation differently. To say

I wanted to take matters in my own hands would be an understatement.

I wanted to loudly voice how I felt. They had done this to my child all because of the color of his skin. Removing my son from that environment could not be done soon enough.

My husband sat me down and recommended we handle the matter with prayer. Deep down, I knew he was right. I prayed, and the answer to that prayer came in the form of the school board superintendent, who recommended my child be transferred to another school in the county.

What was the reason for the transfer? Racial discrimination.

The following year, both my sons were transferred to another school. My husband and I were soon transporting them every day to a school twenty minutes away, right past a school within walking distance.

Transferring to a school with more diversity should have made life easier for my sons. In the beginning, it seemed as if we had made the right choice. I thought things would work out better for my children but lurking beneath the surface was an underlying racial tension not only amongst the faculty at the new school, but the students as well.

In two years, things would drastically change and the injustices this time would be directed towards my other son. It was the calm before the storm. During practice of one of the sporting teams, my son was called over by another player for what seemed like help. The situation was explained to my son and immediately he knew that it was racially motivated and was willing to help address the situation.

Another member of the team looked at my son and stated, "I have the right to call you a n-----!"

Knowing my son was not the type to back down from any challenge, he wanted to address the matter. He explained what was said to a nearby coach who approached them when he saw the commotion. The coach's response was that he had not heard anything—even though he seemed to be within ear reach—and that everyone should get back to practice.

My son simply refused to let this rest quietly. The next day he went back to the African American teammate who had initially called him over for "help." That teammate started to deny the racial slur had been said. Shockingly, my son looked at him in disbelief and questioned him about his sudden change of heart. It baffled him that his teammate could change his mind so quickly, seeing that he was so disturbed by the comments the day before.

Administrators as well as other parents were contacted concerning the racial statements. Amazingly, no one wanted to get involved. We were told to just let it ride, sweep it under the rug, and all would be well.

One African American parent told me that because the children have to go to school together, I should just not worry about it. It pained me that representatives of the Black community would permit injustice to occur just to avoid ruffling someone's feathers. My husband and I were not going to let this go.

Several meetings were scheduled to see if we could resolve the matter. The student handbook for the school stated that there was a zero-tolerance policy for racial instances, and my husband and I learned that instances like this were punishable unless you were of certain cliques or sports teams. To appease us, the school board office selected a former African American employee to investigate the situation. Several students and faculty members were interviewed regarding the racial atmosphere in the school.

What the investigator found out was alarming. He discovered that not only did the White students use racial slurs, but they were heavily used among the Black students as well.

The findings were placed in a report and explained to me and my husband. A copy of the report was given to us, with the names of all the minors redacted. That was the finale. In essence, all the perpetrators were given a slap on the wrist.

As a result of standing up for his fellow African American teammate, my son was constantly pulled into meetings with administrators where he faced the White students who had racially offended him and the other African American teammate. My son told the same story every time. He later shared with me that oftentimes he felt alone. He had been minding his business and was pulled into a situation that not only offended him but resulted in others calling him a liar as though the situation never happened.

Having my sons face racial injustices, and seeing the system built to protect those injustices, had caused me to feel extremely hopeless. The frustration level of my husband and I was through the roof. Of course, my husband was much calmer than I was going through these trials. He felt exactly the same way I did but controlled his emotions differently.

Fury is what I felt. How could people get away with doing this to my children and nothing be done in the form of justice?

As a parent it was hard to watch and it was even harder to control my emotions. It not only angered me, it hurt my heart deeply to watch my sons desperately seek restitution for what had been done to them. No matter what we tried, every avenue was met with a roadblock.

I could never write my story if I felt there was no hope. There are moments when one believes there is nothing you can do to rectify racial injustices. Physically, there was nothing we could do to fix our occurrences but there remained one weapon we had in all these trials. Prayer.

Someone might ask, "What is prayer going to do and how is that going to help?" I truly believe that prayer helps, especially if done with a sincere heart. The Lord may not have changed things in the time frame I desired but He did change them in His own time and in a mysterious way. His work is true, and I believe it wholeheartedly.

I was a very young child when I had the teacher who did not want me to play with my white friends. One might wonder the negative impact that teacher had on my young mind. You would assume her views got worse over the years and that her influence would have spread, but as fate would have it, one of my sons ended up having that same teacher decades later.

My first thought was to have him reassigned to another teacher because I did not want him to experience the same treatment I had, but the Lord instructed me to pray over the situation and pay close attention.

As I watched her interactions with my son, I realized something in her had changed. She no longer displayed the same demeanor towards African Americans as she once had. She truly cared for my son and they became very close throughout the years he was in contact with her. I had witnessed something in her that I thought I would never see in my lifetime.

I have since shared this observation with others and they asked me if I had ever inquired as to why she had changed. My answer was a definite no. What took place within that teacher's heart from the point of my interaction with her to the point in which she was around my son was none of my concern.

She had changed in a positive way and there was no reason for me to discuss something that was no longer relevant. The Lord allowed me to witness this transformation and to learn that even though a person could have a racist attitude, He alone is able to change them. It appears that racial attitudes are a learned behavior but they can be unlearned just as well.

When my son was transferred to another school district for three years, my husband and I agreed racial discrimination was the reason we were transferring him. For each of those years, the school board accepted it. In the meantime, we continued to pray about the overall atmosphere and for a change in the mindset of the administrators. Before my son's senior year in high school, we had to submit the transfer papers as we had previously done. My husband and I filled out the papers the same way we had done before but this time the administrator rejected it because he refused to accept that as a valid reason to be transferred.

My sons were encouraged to return to their former school which was around the corner from our house. Miraculously, they were welcomed back. It was vehemently stated that racism, as it related to them, was not a valid reason anymore for their transfer. Interestingly enough, it was true. They were welcomed back with open arms.

The coach who refused to get ice for my son after his assault also changed. He and my sons ended up having a very good rapport with each other. They enjoyed being on his team and he remained helpful to my sons throughout their final years at that school.

What started out as an adverse situation turned out to be a pleasant one. If I had gone strictly with my feelings and emotions based on my previous experiences, I would have never been able to get past what was done to my sons.

Every person and every circumstance is not the same and should not be treated as such. I had to be led by the Lord in order to know there really was a change in the person and the circumstance. The Lord showed me that people could change, that He could change them.

Not all situations have been healed yet. The last remaining situation is one that leaves me somewhat perplexed. When my sons finally transferred back to their initial school within their district, I still observed some very disturbing events. The attitudes against my sons from the school where the racial slurs had been made remained. The sports team one son had previously played on was even instructed to hurt him. I again had to watch this play out along with other African American parents in the stands. My anger rekindled. I was like a mother grizzly bear protecting her cubs but I still had to work to keep my emotions in check.

From experience, I knew someone who could fix everything. There were a lot of prayers sent up during those days for the acts of vengeance on my son. Little by little, over the years I have watched as the Lord has removed some of those coaches from their positions. Has everything worked out in that situation like I would have wanted? Absolutely not! There is one thing I know for sure; the Lord is in control. He does things in His own time and His own way. He is the final judge—not me.

No matter what racially motivated circumstance I have faced, I can say without a shadow of doubt, if I prayed with the correct spirit and asked with a sincere heart, the Lord has answered my prayers. Even if I am not there to witness it, I know that He is. If you ever worry or ever witness injustice, remember…

Prayer changes things.

In^da Visible

By Mahayana Garcia

When I think about why I fight against racism and discrimination, I am reminded of my own experiences. My parents are from two very different races and cultures but my experiences with discrimination haven't been racial. For a long time, I minimized my own experiences because I didn't think they were as important as all of the other events happening around the world.

I eventually realized I wasn't being fair to myself. I may not know exactly how it feels to be discriminated against because of my physical appearance but I do understand what it feels like to be treated very differently due to something unrelated to my character. Due to this, I feel very strongly about speaking out against any form of racial, sexual, religious and educational discrimination.

When I first started school, I knew there was something different about me. I assumed that it was because I was the new kid in a new school but that feeling never went away. I was a quiet and polite child who loved learning and valued education. I didn't have trouble making friends but had trouble keeping up in class. Somedays I would get distracted no matter how hard I tried to focus. I had to attend after school tutoring, which was no help. My mother requested other special education services but was denied.

I was excited to start middle school because I could finally start playing sports. I had waited since elementary school to join the basketball team. Sixth grade wasn't the best year for me. I had a hard time in my classes, and sometimes felt like I was going to fail. My teachers knew I needed a little extra help with reading and writing but some showed little compassion. Once, I overheard my reading teacher tell another teacher that I was a lazy child. That was the moment I realized that not everyone had my best interest in mind.

Instead of getting upset at my teachers, I was hard on myself. My mother begged the school to provide special education services during elementary school but we were told I would be fine. When I kept failing tests in middle school even after my mother tested me on the material the night before, we tried again to get services. This time my mother insisted. I was taken out of class, sent to another room in the building, and tested. Halfway through, I began to cry excessively. I felt so ashamed of myself because I kept messing up. Soon after my mom was notified of my results—nothing wrong, don't worry, she's got good grades.

Sports, my strength, turned out to be just as bad. When I couldn't follow basic directions because they were being yelled at me, I was told, "You look like a deer in headlights." Benched for no apparent reason, I was lectured, "It's your fault the team isn't winning because you aren't even cheering for your team."

Middle school was one disappointment after another but my mother worked hard to bring up my self-esteem. She persuaded me to enter a foul shooting contest. I won. My mother made me practice 100 foul shots each day. She wanted to teach me that I could improve and succeed with practice and commitment. I became the state champion two years in a row and first runner up another year. That small victory, outside of the school, gave me the little hope I needed to push through.

My high school freshman year was probably the worst of all my experiences in the Jefferson County West Virginia school system. I was expected to read and write at a much more advanced level. No matter how hard I worked, I still received mediocre grades. My mother explained that I had dyslexia but that I could comprehend the material. I wanted to be in the honor's classes but the teacher refused and said, "I feel like you would do better in a class with kids more like you. I just don't quite feel you are fit for honors." I went home and cried for hours. My mother met with the teacher and an administrator. The two claimed that children with disabilities shouldn't be in honor's classes. My mother claimed that the practice of blocking children with disabilities from honors classes was illegal. She demanded that I be allowed into the honors class and it worked.

That was the start of my mother becoming known as the "troublemaker" at my high school, so I only shared the very worst school experiences with her.

Math was even worse. My disability causes me to get anxious during timed tests. Since the school still hadn't provided me with an Individualized Education Plan (IEP), I had no real accommodations. Instead I was put on a plan in lieu of an IEP because the school didn't want to provide proper testing. My first math teacher gave timed reading tests. When my mother complained, I was moved to another class. That teacher had joined the band wagon of those who hated my mother, "the troublemaker." She refused to give me a calculator, claiming there weren't enough. As part of my plan, I was to take tests in a separate, quiet environment. While I was in one room, the teacher wrote the answers to the harder problems on the board for the others in class. Of course, my mother complained and was told that there was nothing wrong with me and I wasn't getting special treatment because my mother worked for the school system. The principal's response was, "Well you have been doing pretty well in the class, so one grade won't be that bad."

My mother again started asking for proper testing. I was tested and again told that I had no disabilities. My mother started receiving threats and was harassed by school staff because of her complaints. My abuse increased.

Even though my history teacher, who was one of the most popular teachers in the school, was told I had trouble spelling, she gave me a spelling question to be answered aloud. All the other students were asked history questions. I was red-faced and embarrassed when I couldn't spell the word under duress. The next day, because my mother questioned the behavior, the teacher pulled me aside and gave me a stern warning that I had thrown him under the bus. The more my mother complained, the more teachers joined in on the bullying. One teacher stopped my mother in the hall and said, "You need to stop going around telling people your daughter has a disability. She is in my daughter's class and my daughter isn't Special Ed."

By my sophomore year, my mother had enough. She found a doctor to test me for dyslexia and had to pay $4000.00 for the specialist. One cold, windy March morning in 2016, we drove to Pennsylvania. I spent the day taking numerous tests and completing questionnaires.

Afterwards, I ran out of the building crying from the frustration and feelings of overwhelm. I cried myself to sleep.

A month later results arrived in the mail. Finally, it was documented that I had Attention-Deficit Hyperactivity Disorder (inattentive type) and Dyslexia, which caused reading and math problems. The report showed that I needed extra time on tests and assignments, a private and quiet testing environment, shouldn't be graded for spelling, couldn't use scantrons for tests, and many other recommendations.

My mother took the test to the school but no one would accept it. The pupil services director claimed that I didn't qualify for services because I wasn't failing, and the counselor told us it wasn't her place to deal with it.

The special education coordinator said she couldn't take the 200-page report. Angrily, my mother took the report to the principal and told her that she either needed to schedule a meeting with us or she would be sued.

The school system continued fighting my mother so she did have to sue them just to give me an IEP. In court, it was revealed they never had completed a proper test, never requested proper documentation from the teachers, never reviewed past test scores, and never did the appropriate observations in any of the three previous tests given over an eight year period.

My mother had to explain to the school system terms like, "Social Promotion" and "Dyslexia." It was pathetic that these leaders knew very little about disabilities. The judge ruled in my favor and granted everything requested, which was minimal. The school system had spent thousands of dollars to fight us over a few accommodations. The judge said she thought it seemed personal against my mother, which was probably why the system refused to follow the judge's directives.

The teachers refused to follow the IEP. It would take another year and the school being placed on a corrective action plan by the State Board of Education before the Board of Education would accept the judge's demands. By then, we'd had enough. My mother had been ostracized by her co-workers, blocked from jobs and promotions, and harassed miserably. The principal tried to keep me from being a member of the National Honor Society and from wearing my club regalia at graduation.

For my senior year, I did most of my classes online as part of the dual enrollment program, just to not have to fight with the teachers anymore.

I am a junior at Shepherd University majoring in Biology and Environmental Science. Sometimes I wish I was playing college sports. I won medals at the state track meets and even made it to the youth Olympics.

I think about what life would have been like if I hadn't quit the volleyball team in high school because the coach was abusive. She belittled me in front of everyone and claimed that I refused to learn my left from right—known issues for dyslexics. Even though I went to states every year for swimming and won medals, I lost my passion for swimming when the coach told people I was an idiot.

I still have trouble speaking up and definitely need a spell checker and calculator, but I understand everything very well. I am living proof that you can't judge a person by their appearances. I think that teachers may have accepted that I had learning problems if I was in a wheelchair or had a hearing aid. Because they couldn't see a disability, in their minds, it didn't exist.

Then there are those who assumed that I had a low IQ because of the dyslexia. I have learned that the people who are paid to be professionals don't always act professional, or even know how to properly execute their jobs.

From all of this, I have learned that people will discriminate, abuse, harass and attempt to destroy others who fight for their rights or the rights of others.

I learned there are many people stuck in the past, who believe if Johnny can't read, he needs to be smacked for being lazy. I have learned that you can't know another person's story by looking at the color of their skin, their job title, their education level, or the stories that others tell about them. We must see others as equally deserving and must provide liberty and justice for all.

Finding Your Voice

By Danielle Gavin

If I had been asked ten years ago what my views on racism, inequality, injustice, police brutality, or any other similar topic that has since been front and center in the media, I would have no idea what to say. I was raised in an upper middle-class family who "didn't see color" and would never flat out tell me," Don't hang around so and so" based strictly off their race, appearance, or socioeconomic status. Even though I was taught to be accepting of everyone, there were always clear expectations of what type of person I should be looking for in a partner. It was made clear that certain family members would have "strong feelings" or "old fashioned views" about who I associated with.

I never witnessed anyone in my family be hateful to anyone, but I never witnessed anyone stand up for, or even acknowledge, that racism was a current issue either. I became more exposed to the real world as I graduated and was on my own but even as a young adult I never thought much about racism. I had learned it existed but didn't know anyone it affected personally. I thought it was enough that I wasn't prejudiced and was kind, and that I treated everyone equally. Sadly, that is *not* enough.

The truth is racism is all around us, from the way our history is taught to the way a Black person can be treated for simply existing. I was completely ignorant to the fact that there were racist police officers. I could not believe that the court system would ever be prejudiced. After all, weren't these people supposed to protect us?

If someone went to jail, they must have committed a crime and deserved to do their time. Maybe once in a while there would be a mistake but those wouldn't ever be intentional, right?

Wrong.

When I began dating my boyfriend, Andre, I was absolutely appalled at the way I would get side-eyed by people seeing us together. Little did I know dirty looks and muttered comments were just the tip of the iceberg. I have witnessed police harass, bait, follow, and belittle Andre just for being black. If I get pulled over by myself, I usually bat a few lashes and get off with a warning and a smile. Every time I have been pulled over with him in the car, I have been pulled out, cuffed, detained, and had to wait for K9s to search my car.

If I did not witness it firsthand, I never would have believed it. He does not have a criminal record, there is never a reason to run his name and assume there would be a problem, but it happens *every* time. Andre is talked down to, questioned about every tattoo or things he is not involved with. He was arrested and held on a five-thousand-dollar cash-only bond for failing to appear in court while he was actually sitting in the courtroom waiting to be called for the case.

I was then questioned for over an hour about where I got the bail money before they would accept it and release him. Andre has been arrested multiple times over warrants that do not exist and been mirandized maybe only once. The scariest time for him was when he was booked in jail for over two weeks for this same non-existent warrant, with no court date in sight. I showed up with our lawyer and proof of the paid ticket and documents from the court date but that did not matter. It was the most helpless feeling ever, knowing the situation was terribly wrong and not being able to do anything about it. Even with proof in their hands, the court still dragged their feet on his release while never attempting to compensate for or admit their mistake.

The police never gave him a hard time until he called them out on profiling him and wrongfully arresting him that first time. Since then, he has become an instant target. We have had to move homes and change vehicles on several occasions because the police would follow him around, just waiting for a reason to harass him. Andre has no reason to be discriminated against. All he has ever been is a positive role model who uplifts his community and improves the lives of countless children through his work. He is profiled and discriminated against simply based on his appearance.

I used to call Andre several times a day. I was terrified he would not come home. Anytime I heard sirens and he was nearby, my heart would stop. This may sound dramatic but when it becomes your life it is terrifying. With all the instances of police brutality circulating through the media and the flawed city police department, it was not unrealistic for me to be afraid every time we saw sirens behind us.

Watching him go through this was the most heartbreaking and eye-opening experience for me in seeing the truth about the world. I used to be the first to say someone was "pulling a race card" or "being dramatic" because I did not understand where they were coming from. Once I began to see how real it was to experience racism and how offensive and degrading it is, I decided I had to do better.

Andre became extremely interested in his culture and history while this was going on and I felt that it was only right to educate myself as well. I strongly believe that people must reflect those they spend their lives with, ready to support them in any battle, understand their demons, and help create their peace. In order to do this, I had to do more than sympathize. I had to empathize. I had to research. I had to listen a lot. I had to learn. I started understanding that terms like "whitewashed" and "white privilege" were not theatrical terms used by people who were trying to get attention, but very real issues.

I know there are terrible people in the world who refuse to see the good and cannot open their mind to the beauty of everyone but I would like to hope the reason that people are less than understanding about racism is because they just don't understand. If I can choose to open my eyes and better myself, anyone can.

I encourage everyone to read deeper into history than what we are taught in school. Do research about our country, about slavery, about culture and where different people came from. Read about current events, and how frequent there are issues of police brutality, falsified evidence, and crooked court cases. Look up names like Breonna Taylor, Eric Gardner, Sandra Bland, George Floyd, Wayne Jones. Search for people's experiences and testimonies that are shared on social media All you need to do is look. The information is out there if we open our minds and dig deeper.

Becoming a mother to black children opened my eyes to a different type of prejudice. I never imagined the hatred some people could direct toward a child simply because their mother and father are different races. I have only had a handful of instances where someone has taken their misery out on our family but becoming a mother to black babies who would grow into black men puts a whole new fear in my heart. I had watched their dad get profiled and harassed and it broke my heart in so many ways because I knew him, and I knew it was wrong.

I did not realize how different it would impact me when I was considering my children being in those situations. I can raise my sons to be the most respectful and well behaved boys ever. I can ensure they get good grades. I can keep them in activities and out of the street. I can make sure they are educated on how to conduct themselves if stopped by police or in a confrontation with someone unkind. I can do all the right things but I cannot guarantee that I will not get a phone call that my son was wounded or worse because a closed-minded bigot got on the wrong side of a trigger.

I cannot guarantee that someone will not perceive my black sons as a threat based on their appearance or style. I would die for my children, no question about it but I cannot be with them every second of every day. It is a hard thought to stomach that a child would lose their life to senseless violence, but it happened to Tamir Rice and Trayvon Martin.

This war does not spare children. What age do I transition from police being "good guys" and the world being a safe place to telling them the truth about all the monsters that surround us? My son said a police officer looked scary the other day, and I hate to admit that it felt wrong to correct him and say "No, police are nice" when I shouldn't have hesitated to make that statement. What age do I start talking to them about the color of their skin? What age do I take away the toy guns? What age do I tell them the truth about the struggle they will always face solely because of their skin? These are not questions that a mother should have to ask, but these are discussions in our household.

I have learned a lot throughout the last decade. I have done a lot of soul searching. I have had a lot of hard conversations with myself. I learned that it does not matter what kind of environment you are raised in or what you previously thought was right, the point of life is to grow and do better.

We have such a huge source of information at our fingertips, it would be simply irresponsible and selfish to not take time to continue to learn. The most important idea I have learned is that ignoring the issue and being blind to injustice is the worst thing one can do. It is humbling and embarrassing to realize you have been blind to things that are so obvious and that instead of doing the right thing, you have been a part of the problem.

Silence is part of the problem. You are not making a change if you are not speaking up. It is imperative to see color. Even if color does not matter to you or you are a kindhearted person who does not have a hateful bone in your body, you have to see color. You must be aware of the power you have as a white person.

White privilege does not mean you have life easy because you are white, or that you do not work for what you have. White privilege means you are automatically perceived as an equal. White privilege means you do not have to fight as hard for the same basic rights everyone should have. Know that your presence could directly influence the way a person is treated and you see someone being treated wrongly, speak up. Correct the people who are spreading false information and learn facts to share instead. Teach your white children to watch out for my Black sons, because police are not the only authority figures who misuse their positions. Schools can be dangerous too.

Support the Black community. Become educated on their struggles and you will also learn about the beauty of their culture, the warmth of their acceptance, their powerful spirit, and the passion so many exude. Seeing differences because of color is not a bad thing but hating someone because of color is.

Unity is necessary to move forward in the world. This issue has been ignored for years and it's time to address it. I know that I personally have made it a goal to spread love, knowledge, and acceptance. While I know it is impossible to reach everyone, and that some people will remain closed minded, I refuse to stop trying to make a difference. My partner or my children could be the next news story and I cannot sit back and be okay with that. I will channel my fear and passion into positivity and will continue to fight, march, and speak alongside my family to be a voice for those who no longer have one.

Ignorance in Innocence

By Angel Holmes

"Ignorance is bliss" is a term that I've heard many times, but I never really thought deeply into its meaning. I believe this concept is abundant right now as issues such as police brutality, inequality, and hate crimes are just a few of the major fights we are dealing with in the Black and brown communities. Those around us who it is not affecting are not feeling the same impact as we are.

My purpose in life is helping children. Children are innocent. Children are not born with the trait of hate. Hate is taught. Many people believe younger children are spared from these issues, but they also are affected by hate and inequality. Some of them realize, and some do not because of how early it can start.

It is important to me that I use my knowledge and experiences to help the innocent understand that we must be kind and respectful towards each other, and that although we might be taught to hate , it does not matter what color we or our friends are in the crayon box. We must show love and compassion for one another.

* * *

"Why have you been avoiding us?" I asked my friend.

"I don't want to say," she said.

"What do you mean?" I replied back.

"Well," she began, "my parents found the note in my bag from Derek and got mad. They told me I couldn't play with you anymore. They said I could be friends with Black people, but I could never date one. They said I went too far. I'm sorry but I miss you guys." I watched her turn and walk away.

I was nine.

* * *

My friends and I loved to play outside. We rode bikes, climbed trees, and had water balloon fights. One day, we were riding around the neighborhood when Tony remembered he needed to do something for his mom at the house. We rode to their house and then walked to the door. When we got there, our other friend Adam walked in the house, the rest of us were following suit. "You can't come into our house," said Tony.

"What do you mean?" asked Joe.

"Exactly what I said", said Tony, "we're not allowed to have Black people inside of our house."

"You're joking, right?" I replied.

"No, I'm not joking," said Tony, "I don't know when our parents will be back home, so you all have to wait outside. The rest of you can come inside though."

"You all are Mexican and some of your family is illegal, but they don't like Black people?" I asked him.

"I don't make the rules guys, I just follow them."

I stood outside with my two other friends Joe and Harlee, confused as we watched everyone else walk inside the house.

I was eleven.

* * *

It was volleyball season, one of the best times of the year. My team and I walked into the opposing team's gym and got nothing but stares. We walked past them, focusing on the game ahead, and sat in the corner.

We began to see flashes, kids running towards us, and then away. Eventually, one of my teammates yelled out, "What the heck is going on and what are you all doing?"

One of the girls looked at my friend Kendra and responded with, "Can I touch your skin?"

My friend quickly looked at me and said, "Excuse me?"

"Well," said the same girl, "we just have never seen one in person."

"Never seen a what?" asked Kendra.

"A brown person," she said with a serious, straight face.

Kendra, the rest of my team, and I were dumb founded.

"What do you mean you've never seen a brown person?" I asked her.

"There are no brown people here. We have only seen them on TV and movies. We didn't mean any harm. We are just so excited to see some in real life."

"They're not safari animals," said Alyssa.

"I know, I know," the girl said. "I just think it's cool that I've finally seen a brown skinned person in real life. I can't wait to tell my family."

The group of girls turned and walked away. We were left not knowing how to feel. Should we have been offended, or should we feel good that we were able to be her first experience with brown skinned people in real life? Either way, it was a very awkward situation that was purely based on the color of my skin.

My team had one more game to win before we made it to the championship basketball game the same year. We were warned to keep our heads down, play our game, and then get back on the bus. We got to the school and were greeted with silence (besides our own fans of course). We walked in and instantly felt hate. Not one person from the other school looked like over half of our team. We were booed and called names. The words were not only from kids but from adults as well.

It was a very odd situation that we weren't used to coming from a small, loving town. The game continued, and the players on the court were just as bad as the crowd. Names were called, elbows were thrown, and altercations began. We were then escorted into our locker room. After our coach talked to the referees, we went back out to finish the game. We won that game but all I remember from that victory is how much hate we faced from the time we walked in to the time we walked back out to the bus.

I was thirteen.

* * *

Racism happens within the Black community as well. We struggle with a battle called colorism which was started back in slave days. The definition of colorism is "Prejudice or discrimination against individuals with darker skin tones, typically among people of the same ethnic group or race." During slavery, when the masters would rape the slaves, they would end up with mulatto or lighter children. Those children were treated better and given more privileges than the dark-skinned slaves. Things such as working inside, allowed educational advantages, or even given freedom.

This created interracial hierarchy and allowed Mulattos to capitalize on freedoms by using their literacy to get into better economic statuses after emancipation (Reece, 2018). These things started the lighter skin is better than darker skin separation amongst our own race.

Growing up in a small town the option to date someone of the same race is small due to size. I never thought that at some point I wouldn't be able to date someone of the same race because they felt as though my skin color made me lesser of a woman or a less suitable mate. A skin color that is shared by many of their moms, grandmas, sisters, and themselves.

It was my first night as a college freshman. I had just left a concert at my university and decided to meet up with some new friends. My new friend Chanel was amazing. She was a sweet, bubbly, beautiful brown skinned girl, and was also on the cheerleading team. She was excited to go out that night because we were going to see Scott.

Scott was a nice, brown skinned boy who played on the football team. She met him at an athlete meeting during the summer Freshman orientation. She said they kept in touch, and she couldn't wait to finally spend some time with him.

When we got to the party, we were met with the sounds of music and laughter. It was my first college outing, and I was so excited. I remember getting some punch. Then, everyone sat down in a circle to talk and get to know each other better. I remember everyone discussing our majors and minors. We discussed where we were from, and who played what sport. It was going a lot better than I thought it would but then it quickly started to go bad.

We heard a conversation between two guys. They were arguing about a girl that they both wanted to get to know. I remember Bryan telling Chaz, "well how about we just see who she wants?"

That's when everyone started talking about who they had their eyes on. I was very shy and awkward. I silently sat in the background listening. The group started to get rowdy.

"I don't want no dark-skinned girl," yelled out Chris.

The group followed in response:

"OOOOOOO NOOOOO!"

"EW!"

"HELL NO!"

"What do you mean you don't want no dark-skinned girl?" my most outspoken friend, Kiki, yelled.

"Listen," said Ethan, "they're cool to be friends with but that's it."

"I only like light skinned and white girls," shouted Garrett.

"Who are you to be saying who you will talk to?" Kiki shouted. "You're not too hot yourself, telling somebody you don't like them because of how they look on the outside, big boy."

Everyone laughed except Garrett.

"Yeah, doesn't feel too good does it," Kiki said as she sat back down.

"Either way," yelled D, "White is the only way for me."

"I agree." said Scott. "I would never date you, or you, or you" he continued as he pointed at Chanel.

My heart broke instantly knowing how much she liked him. I looked her in her eyes and saw her trying to act unphased.

"I'll be right back. I'm going to get some more punch," she said softly as she quickly walked away.

My friend Kelsi and I followed to check on her. I saw a small tear run down her face.

"Are you ok sweetie?" Kelsi said.

"So, he's just been playing me this whole time? I am such a great person."

"Yes, you are! You don't need any of those fools to know that," I said. We hugged and went back over.

Kiki, of course, was yelling. "Your moms, grandmas, and sisters are Black women. How can you feel this way?"

That experience was my first night in college.

Why I Stand

I was eighteen

* * *

One of my favorite people in this entire world is my father. He was a collegiate baseball player and now lives his best life and has been a teacher and coach for over 15 years. During his later years, I have watched my father work hard to accomplish many degrees overtime. I have been his sidekick my whole life. I have also followed in his footsteps and become a coach.

One night, I was standing in the hall with my dad in between basketball games. As we stood there, a woman from the opposing team walked up to my dad and started talking to him (which isn't uncommon because both of my parents can become friends with anyone we encounter). I went to talk to some students inside the cafeteria and to get some water. When I came out, another woman walked up to my dad. She told him he needed to go put paper towels in the bathroom and clean it up.

I remember feeling my face torte as I looked up at my father. "You are the janitor, aren't you?" She asked him.

My mouth opened in disbelief. My father is the nicest, sweetest man, most of the time but if you make him mad, it gets ugly.

I saw the look on his face, and I was instantly worried about what would happen next.

He looked at her and said, "I'm not the janitor. Why would you think that? Is it because I'm Black?"

I remember my eyes bugging out of my head. I was scared for him. I too was insulted by her words.

Jumbled statements rolled out of her mouth until she finally got out, "No, not at all. I just-"

"You just what?" he asked her. "You just assumed that the Black man was the janitor? I know." He calmly said, "I am a highly educated teacher. I have more degrees than you will ever see in your life."

The lady quickly scurried away. I looked at my dad. I could not believe that just happened. He told me "People always think I'm the janitor. Black guy always has to be the janitor."

The blatant racism was a lot to handle. To see another say such hurtful words to someone I love so much made me so upset. He hugged me and said, "Bubba, it's ok. I know I'm smarter than she'll ever be. It's not the first time, and probably won't be the last."

We walked back into the game like nothing had happened. It may not have phased him but it had an impact on me. I knew how hard he worked for his degrees and how important his role is in our community, yet this random person could just come and try to deliberately diminish it all. I realized that we weren't as far from racism as I had thought.

I was twenty-two.

* * *

"I want to go to Africa," "Can I go to Africa?" and "What is Africa like?" are comments that I would hear from one of my students often. It was Pre-K, and kids say just about anything.

"Why don't you get a book about Africa, and tell me some things you see?" I asked him.

Carter continued with these comments for weeks. We read books, looked up animals, and just dove right into his newfound fascination. One morning, I heard him speak. I just continued to make sure the class was settled. I told the kids to sit down on the rug so we could begin class. As we began, Carter said, "Ms. Angel, are you listening to me? I said, 'did you know that White means power?'"

"No, it doesn't, it's a color!" shouted another kid quickly.

"That's what I told them," he said. "I said it's a color like green and blue."

"That's exactly right," I said. "Who told you that anyway Carter?"

"My Pawpaw and Mimi!" he replied. His comment hit me like a brick.

I thought about that comment for the rest of the day. During nap time, I told my assistant Viv and she had a funny look on her face.

"What's wrong?" I asked her.

"Well," she began, "his family isn't very modern." She continued telling me about how she'd known his family for quite some time, and that they have had racist tendencies in the past.

"What do you mean??" I asked her.

"For example," she began, "he was supposed to change classrooms due to his family moving homes. Classrooms are based on location. When they found out his teacher was black, they made excuses until they allowed them to stay with me saying he needed me for support. Last year, he had a Hispanic teacher that they wouldn't even say hello to. They told him he didn't have to listen to her. Things are different with you though. They have asked about you."

"Asked about me for what reason?" I asked her.

"He is very close to you. He comes home and talks about you. They are being forced to be more open because he really loves you."

I had never thought about how close we really were. I had never really thought about his negative comments.

I remember the first time he yelled, "I'm not sitting by no people like that!" at lunch.

"We're all friends here. What if they don't want to sit by you? Did you think about that?" I had asked him.

The situation rested heavy on my mind for days. It went from just my mind to also hurting my soul.

They hated me based purely on my skin color. They had never met me, but already wanted nothing to do with me. It hurt me more because he was so little, yet so much hate was consistently spewing out of him. How could someone be able to exclaim, "I will not sit beside people like you," yet not be able to write their own name? How can you not yet recognize all your colors but say 'white means power?'

There was so much evil and ignorance coming out of such an innocent little mouth. This child was being spoon-fed hate before he could even understand what he was being taught.

It was hard for me to internalize the hate knowing the backstory of the family. I tried to tell myself, "I know that he has gone through so much in such a short time but does that make it okay?" I tried to give them an excuse for hating me. There must be something more to it, I would tell myself. I think a lot of us always say "There must be something more. There's no way that people are still hating me for the color of my skin." The situation also made me angry. "How dare they?" I'd say to myself. I am a wonderful, educated member of my community. I constantly do things to try and make life better for so many, yet a family that has not lived their lives on the straight and narrow dare to try and belittle me based on my skin?

I had only one choice. I had to love and to teach. I had to do everything in my power to make as much of a positive impact as a Black woman on his life as I could before he left my class.

I am twenty-seven.

* * *

These are just a few of the encounters that have stuck with me the most over time. I am one check away from being the most hated demographic in this world. I am a Black woman. Though the most hated, Black women are the most educated demographic. I was raised by a strong Black family.

My parents were married before my sister and I were born and are still married today. We are also their only children. I have been blessed to have many strong Black role models on both sides of my family. My grandmothers, Jenny Miller and Edy B, were like none other. Just say their names, and everyone's first thoughts are "Loving, but don't take no mess." Their values passed down to my parents and their siblings. Seeing them be so outspoken has given me the strength and confidence to break out and speak up even more at this point in my life. My family members are all pillars of the community. We are teachers, coaches, lawyers, doctors, first responders, authors, chefs, and so much more. They have pushed me to continually strive to be the best I can be and to do whatever it is I set my mind to. I have never felt like I was unable to do something because of the color of my skin.

In more recent times, however, hate has been so much more prevalent. My purpose was made apparent to me very early on in my life - to work with kids and help them to get as far as they can.

As a teacher, you must go above and beyond with students. Some kids are not blessed to have the role models or the love I had growing up. This means that it is sometimes my job to teach respect, morals, values, kindness, strength, and love.

I feel as though now more than ever it is my job to teach beyond the books and court. A lot of the hate that is spewed from children comes from their ignorance on the topics. They are just repeating what they have been taught through a long cycle of ignorance. When you ask them why they think the way they do, they have no justification. The kids that yell, "Trump 2020" or "Build that wall" have no political views to back it up. It is simply them replicating what they have seen or heard.

It is my job to educate both sides. We must educate the ignorant students so that they can one day say, "I'm sorry I didn't know," or "I didn't understand." It is okay to not be educated on a topic, but it isn't okay to continue the ignorance once informed. I believe that once we know better, we can do better.

I also want to educate and encourage kids who are afraid to speak up. They must know that it is okay to speak up for what they believe in. It is very easy to be discouraged due to seeing situations such as Colin Kaepernick or the continuous no convictions of the police after brutality cases. They need to feel safe and confident standing up for what they believe is right. If I can use my position to make a difference in just one child's life, I feel as though I'm fulfilling my purpose.

That is why I am determined to use my voice and experiences to help make the changes in the world that I want to see. I will continue to fight for equality, love, and respect for all. Beginning the process with the children I work with. I will continue to combat the ignorance that is forced upon the innocent.

In the Face of Adversity

By Faith Holmes

Growing up, I never experienced racism that surpassed microaggressions. I had gotten used to the comments that my white peers made towards me, such as, "You're so pretty for a Black girl!" or "You're way smarter than I thought you would be!" The day that changed was August 12, 2017. I began to watch the livestream of white supremacists and Neo-Nazis terrorizing people in my own city. One thought that emerged and remained at the forefront of my mind: the violence against Black people that has happened for hundreds of years and continues to happen every single day.

Images like Eric Garner's brutal death, and DeAndre Harris' unjust abuse popped into my mind. In my small hometown of Charlottesville, Virginia, the apparent racism in our country was right in my face. I watched terrorists abuse innocent people in the same streets that I walk down with my friends. Although these types of events were no secret to me, seeing it happen in my own city completely changed the ways I view the world around me.

In the face of adversity, there are two options: fight for what is right or simply comply. I made the choice to fight for what is right. I have never been one to stand by idly in the presence of wrongdoing, and this instance was no different. As a Black woman, I knew that I could not stand by and allow the disrespect endured by my ancestors every day of their lives to continue in mine.

I choose to stand because I have the privilege to do so, which is not something that I take lightly. When people say, "Black Lives Matter," I never question whether this includes my Black life.

There are many issues within the Black community that have caused and continue to cause further divide. One of the biggest issues is colorism. Colorism is defined as "prejudice or discrimination against individuals with a dark skin tone, typically among people of the same ethnic or racial group" (Merriam Webster). On social media, there is a large amount of hate directed toward dark skin women specifically, and as a Black woman with lighter skin this is something I have the privilege of not experiencing. As a result, it is my duty to use my privilege to intervene when I see colorism occurring. Another issue within the Black community is transphobia. When we say, "Black Lives Matter," it means that *all* Black lives matter. There are many occasions when people pick and choose which Black lives they feel are worthy of mattering, but as a cis-gender woman I choose to stand for all Black lives.

In order to truly fight for equality and justice, it is important to recognize my own privilege, which allows me to do so.

In my plight to become an activist, I have felt an array of emotions. The summer before my senior year I decided to use my pain to fuel my purpose. All of the hurt, anger, and confusion were finally becoming useful and would benefit more than just myself.

My endeavor began when I began an internship at the Jefferson School African American Heritage Center, the first Black high school in Charlottesville, Virginia. In 2013, the building became a city space dedicated to authentically telling the history of the Black community in Charlottesville. During my internship, I spent 9 weeks of the summer engaging in primary source research I would later use to develop my own tour of the Center. At the start of my journey, I went through a handful of learning crises as I was presented new information which made me realize that I need to take a stand. The beginning of making real change starts with education, not only of oneself but everyone around them. I could not let my 9 weeks of intensive research go to waste. It is my duty to hold myself accountable for turning my knowledge into something bigger than just my thoughts.

As my internship came to a close, I knew it was time to take my work a step further and continue to make an impact on the people around me. I had learned at the Jefferson School African American Heritage Center the importance of Black Student Unions. Black Student Unions were founded in order to create safe spaces for Black people and allies while simultaneously bringing awareness and working to solve social injustices.

I took the initiative to found the first Black Student Union at my school, Albemarle High. I wanted to take a stand within my own school so everyone would feel heard and represented. Albemarle High School takes pride in the fact that the school is over 15% Black but when I looked around my classes I was not surrounded by people who looked like me. I was not surrounded by people who knew what it was like to be a Black woman in Charlottesville, Virginia. I was not surrounded by people who knew what it was like to be Black in America. Forming a Black Student Union was a place I could educate the people around me and provide a safe space for Black students to express their thoughts and opinions.

Initially the Black Student Union got backlash from some of the white teachers and students who felt it was unfair, but I did not let this get to my head. I knew I needed to take a stand. What is right will always be right, regardless of how people may feel about it. I took a stand because in a predominately white space like Albemarle High there are too many cases of racism and microaggressions that are swept under the rug. There are too many non-Black people who do not understand why a Black Student Union is important.

I chose to use my voice and knowledge to create something that will be beneficial to Black students during their time at Albemarle High School.

Even though the school year came to an abrupt end and the Black Student Union did not get to fulfill all of our goals, I knew my work could not and would not end here. As protests began to break out across the country, I immediately wanted to plan one in Charlottesville. Initially I was nervous to plan a protest in a city where racially charged violence was so familiar but I had the support from the members of the Black Student Union and other activists from Charlottesville.

It took us only three days to plan the protest and it was a huge success. I decided to take a stand by forming a peaceful protest because my freedom is by no means free. My ancestors fought every day of their lives so that I could be where I am today.

Abuse of Power

By Teresa L. Holmes

Since the age of five, I have been hell-bent and determined to enter places and occupy spaces that were not necessarily built for me, or at least that is what some thought. I had no clue what racism or discrimination was at that point, or that God was preparing me at an early age for what was to come.

Kindergarten in those days was not mandatory but a friend and I learned a class would be held locally and we both wanted to attend. The other girls who would be present did not look like us. It was our skin tone that was different. To my friend and me it was inconsequential but our parents and the other adults in our lives did not see it that way.

They had endured their own personal struggles with racism and injustices and were aware of other issues beyond what had affected them directly. They knew how difficult things were and felt that getting us into a class that was particularly being held for whites would be next to impossible.

I was too young to understand the social dominance theory, which indicated that the non-melanated skin tone of the other little girls who would be in that class made them better than me and my friend. All I knew is I wanted to attend school in the little church surrounded by the big trees that I passed every day as I went to get penny candy from the hardware store on the main street. My parents just had to find a way.

I realize now that not giving up until my name was on that kindergarten attendance roll was my first attempt at attaining equality and claiming my God-given space. I used my voice and pleaded my case until I got the results I wanted.

There would be many more occasions throughout my lifetime where my fundamental rights to navigate this earth without prejudices and injustices would be compromised by those who felt superior to me.

These types of thoughts and subsequent actions are the very reason this book is in print. Whether it is bred in the bone of the oppressors or carefully taught, racism is still running rampant to this very day, far more openly now than I can remember in my 62 years of living. The reasons may vary from person to person. Whether it be distrust, fear (of loss of power), loathe, or something else entirely, racism is a choice each person makes.

It is apparent now that I have either been blind to the dominance theory that some of my "friends," colleagues, and other associates hold, or they disguised it quite well. Either way, they cannot carry thoughts and ideals about being controlling, prevailing, and more powerful than another group of individuals and remain a prevalent part of my life. This is where I draw a line in the sand.

It is also evident that each experience and connection up to this point in my life has been strategically planned by God. It was all a part of Him getting me to where I need to be to effectively carry out my assignment. This book is a part of it.

The preparation for my assignment actually started in my kindergarten class where I met a little ginger-haired girl named Becky.

We became good friends and remained so from kindergarten through high school. My family got to know hers well, and at a time when I needed him later in life, the patriarch of her family took me by the hand, offered me guidance and used his influence to help me gain employment for the Federal Government's Student Program, and several other positions after that one.

It was in that very place that I would experience extreme unjustness and impartiality. This time it was at the hands of a manager who felt my desire to take advantage of upward mobility and career development programs, available to each employee, should not be allowed. The "reasoning" made absolutely no sense to me. She felt because none of the other team members chose to participate, I should not participate either. To her it was putting me at an advantage over them.

I reminded my manager it was up to the other staff to also take advantage of the programs if interested. Their decisions to not do so should have had no bearing on me. Still, she felt quite differently.

Subsequently, it took me several meetings with upward management and an Equal Employment Opportunity filing to be granted access to the programs that should have been readily available. They were in place for a reason, for expansion and career advancement, which was the ultimate goal for me.

My persistence set off a firestorm of attacks against me. Everything I did was picked apart even though I had been performing the same duties at an exceptional level for several rating periods. When it was time for my promotion, I had to fight for it even thought I had earned it.

When I finally reached the level where my next step would be to apply for the manager, I was told by a team member and ally that it might be an issue. The manager had made it clear to everyone else on our team that she would not be retiring if there was any chance of me filling that vacancy. She disliked me so much that she would postpone such a significant event in her life just to spite me.

She was a disgrace to the power she had been given as a top-level manager but I refused to make that problem mine. I knew I had to make a move. I refused to allow anyone to have that type of influence over me or my career.

As He always does, God had a plan. A former manager from the agency I worked had a Service Director vacancy. She felt I would be a perfect fit.

After interviewing and being accepted, I had a decision to make. The position was 12 hours away from home in a place where I only knew one person. Ultimately, I made the commitment to go.

It turned out to be one of the best choices I have ever made. I went from working for a manager who tried to hold me back to having full support, an unlimited budget, and permission to hire as many team members as I felt needed.

Things went great for almost six years, then the manager who hired me accepted another position, and the new manager despised me from the beginning.

"You're light skinned so you may be okay here in the South," were the first words he spoke to me. No hello. No handshake. Nothing else to accompany his despicable words. Racism was not new to me at that point but those words were quite disturbing coming from an executive leader of an extremely diverse workforce.

It did not take long for him to start disbanding the programs I had built and making changes that went against regulatory processes and procedures, with the expectation that I endorse them. I had worked too hard to get to where I was and would not put my career in jeopardy. Not for him or for anyone. Again, it was time to make a move.

My next position as a full-time traveling consultant turned out to be a temporary stop along my journey but was extremely instrumental in leading me to my true purpose: to effect change through storytelling. I was able to travel the country building relationships and collecting resources for what was to come next.

When people asked me why I chose storytelling as my business focus, I was initially unable to articulate properly. All I knew was that it felt right in my soul.

Now I know the why. Through storytelling, others and I can build bridges that connect people through their struggles. Our stories help us recognize our realities and bring us together to enhance and create a more just and fair place to live.

Thus, here we are. Each contributor in this book shares their realities, and though they may be different, we all strive to live together justly and equally.

Our struggles are all real. Our challenges are massive. We each know that our stories can have a significant impact in the fight for social justice. Together we will be boots on the ground, stepping toward the solution for racism and other very critical issues that negatively impact our communities.

The Pain of Love

By Donna Joy

As I watched the television broadcast of the procession escorting John Lewis's sacred, lifeless body over the Edmund Pettus bridge, I was reminded of my own horrific experience of racism while crossing a bridge. The same recollection happened when I watched the video recording of George Floyd being murdered, face on the ground, arms behind his back, desperate for breath, only because of someone else's ignorance, rage, and hate.

It was a Saturday morning, like any other day. I too was 25 and worked as a special education teacher in Baltimore City. I had previously dreamed of studying physics and engineering. I was an introverted problem solver in love with the natural laws of the universe. At Southwestern High School, I won an award for science and the "Best Student" award. I had a 100% average in trigonometry. Einstein was my hero. Until I read his biography, I never knew anyone who thought like me. I was happy dealing with abstract concepts, not people or their problems. That changed when I started college at Towson University.

My history teacher, Mr. Chenoweth, drove me an hour away from the slum and into a whole new world. When we got to the campus, he said, "This is a college and you need to go here." I had no idea what I was getting into. I was the only person from my neighborhood to go to college. It was a culture shock, having never seen so many white people in my life. They all looked alike, dressed alike, and had the same values. The girls had bobbed haircuts and the boys wore alligator shirts and dockers. Growing up in a 99% black, inner-city, West Baltimore slum, I had always felt like an unwelcome alien because I was known as a "white cracker" and a "white honky bitch." I was someone they could take their frustrations out on; I was someone they could blame *Roots* on.

During the broadcast, Bob Shiffrar described how John Lewis had sat at a lunch counter and allowed himself to be beaten. I remembered the times at Harlem Park Junior High—bars on the windows, barbed wire fences, chains locking us in and keeping more violence out— while swarms of Black kids smacked the few little white kids in the back of the head as they rushed to get to class. I remember each time there were usually too many for me to fight and survive, except for the times when a single black boy would grab my butt and I would hit him with whatever I had as hard as I could. I was the one suspended because I hit first.

Every day I went back to school, I was suspended again, usually for fighting or cutting class. "Trouble again, Joy?" Mr. Day would say while he wrote my pass to go home, "Can't come back without your mother." I have no idea the number of fights I was in or the number of times I was suspended. Students were not allowed on city streets without a school pass or they would be arrested. I once stole a pack of early dismissal passes from Mr. Day's desk. It was only fair, I thought. I didn't think I deserved to be suspended. "If I was Black, it would be the boy suspended," became my motto. My friend Ruth and I were able to use the passes to cut class for most of the year since she was so good at forging signatures. Ruth and I used to sneak in the bathroom to smoke cigarettes too.

On one occasion, three Black girls came in and cornered us. They taunted us with various comments about being white trash and wouldn't let us leave. As they moved closer to our faces, one asked angrily, "Did you watch *Roots* last night?" Ruth responded that she had. The girl responded, "I bet you liked it, didn't you?" Ruth said "no" as I stood quiet, nervously watching and waiting for the first one to throw a punch or pull out a weapon. Thank God a teacher smelled the cigarette smoke from the hall. She opened the bathroom door and yelled in, "Anyone in there? You put them cigarettes out and get to class. I'm locking up." The girls quickly ran out and we were saved from a potentially bloody battle, or worse.

White kids had been killed and raped at my school. A few students had been killed for their sneakers. That's how my sister, Kim, was allowed to quit school in the ninth grade. Three against two would have been much better odds than usual though, I thought. Each time I was harassed or bullied, I would repeat the same mantra in my 12 year old mind, "One day I will be in a better place and you will still be here in this slum with the rats and roaches, poverty, welfare checks, miserable heat penetrating from the black tar streets and the stench from the dumpsters near the fish markets." The more I endured abuse, the more I transformed my anger and rage into fuel to motivate me to escape poverty and the hell that came with it.

When I found myself at the suburban, white, Towson University, it was an even worse experience. Even though I had been inducted into the National Honor Society and won so many awards while in high school, one would have thought I had never been. I had no idea what a comma was used for, had no math or research skills, and was oblivious in many classroom conversations due to my cultural upbringing.

I remember an English literature class discussion about cattails. My only frame of reference were the tails that bully kids would cut from the alley cats in the garbage that fought stray dogs for food. By the end of the class, I discovered that cattails were a type of plant. The only plants we had were the cherry trees all along the city streets that had been planted a hundred years before.

The professors seemed to cover everything I learned during my 12 years in the slum schools in only one day. I was shocked to discover that we were expected to read huge textbooks by ourselves. I thought that we would get in groups and read portions together. I had only ever used one textbook. It was a 40-year-old trigonometry book that we copied homework problems from. Academically, I was at a huge disadvantage, but because I now had the same color skin as 99% of those around me, I was expected to be more like the whites.

I wore ragged clothes from the inner-city thrift stores, spoke in slang, and used profanity to emphasize my feelings. "Wow! There is a word for that," I used to think when I discovered the "white" language. Meanwhile, my schoolmates only seemed concerned about whether their parents would give them a car for Christmas or an exotic vacation for spring break. I worried if I would have that one dollar to catch the bus back through the city streets and back to the slum that I called home.

I worried about whether the next morning would be the day I would be jumped by a gang of angry, racist, Black girls or if a 6 foot tall Black boy would grab my butt or worse, while waiting at the bus stop, near the dirty, rat and roach infested projects.

If I had a foreign accent, they would have accepted that I was different, chalking it up to me just being from a different country. In a sense, we were worlds apart. When I graduated high school, there were no parents in the audience to cheer for me. I had been living on my own since I was 16. I had raised my siblings until my mother was released from prison and moved them 500 miles away, ripping out my heart in the process. Classmates talked about exciting plays during college football games while I would share about the murder, or shooting, I witnessed the same night.

The distance between us grew. Their glares pushed me further away. One of the most profound lessons I learned was discovering that white people could say things without meaning them. Where I came from, you knew from a mile away what was on someone's mind. You could spot someone who was up to no good—a would-be attacker. People spoke from their hearts. It was mostly anger but it was real. It took me many years to understand the tricks whites would use to hide their feelings.

I wasn't Black and I was clearly not white. I hadn't only been cheated of an education but I had to learn to maneuver a whole new world. I changed my major to education and was determined to not let this experience happen to anyone else. I was going to teach kids from the Baltimore slum how to escape poverty.

Perhaps it was seeing the counter where John Lewis sat that reminded me of the time I worked at a Black owned and operated Kentucky Fried Chicken restaurant a few miles from the university. I worked the window and the front register most of the time. When business was slow, the cashiers had to clean. I often wondered what provoked the black manager to hand me a two-foot high pink, plastic child's broom one day and force me to sweep the dining room. When I asked why I had to use the completely inappropriate broom, he said, "Joy, I bet you've never had to work a day in your life." I didn't have words for him. I knew I had worked my entire life. As I swept, he smiled, watching me and my mind drifted to my earliest memories of backbreaking work. I remembered Saturdays when my older sister and I would have to lug large, green, industrial garbage bags filled with the clothes of six people, six city blocks to the laundromat.

At four years old, I could only take one step while struggling to carry the two huge bags. My stepfather stood in the doorway and peaked his head around the frame to watch us walk until we turned the corner. If I was ever caught dragging a bag, I would be yelled at, potentially beat, or made to stand in the corner for hours as he smiled watching me.

The laundromat was usually hot, often filled with sketchy people, and always smelled of urine. I remember an older girl there who had a clever way of making the machines work without having to pay. She taught us to put scotch tape around a coin, insert it, turn the knob to start the machine, and pull the taped coin back out.

With the extra money, my sister would buy us ice creams or sodas from the corner store.

On my fifth birthday my sister wanted to use the money to buy me a little "Dawn Doll." We walked up to Murphy's Dime Store on West Baltimore Street, three blocks from our house, but the doll was sold out. My sister said she would buy me one the next week when they were back in stock. As we were halfway home from the store, a Black girl, bigger than me and my nine-year-old sister, jumped out in front of us, held a knife in my face, and asked for our money. Kim responded, "We don't have any money." I said, "Yes, Kim, you have the dollar." The girl demanded it, saying she would cut us if we did not give it to her. She grabbed the dollar bill and ran away out of sight up the alley. I felt so stupid. I felt bad that Kim lost her dollar because I was so naïve. I never had a doll after that.

As I continued sweeping, I remembered all the days before and after school when my sister and I cleaned the house. After dinner, we had to wash, dry, and put away the dishes. My stepfather would come in to inspect. "Nope, it's not clean, take out all the dishes, pots and pans, bowls, and platters. Wash dry, and put them away five times," he demanded. He wouldn't say what was wrong, only that they were not clean. Many nights we would stay up late recleaning the dishes. Eventually, I learned to be passive aggressive. I saw a small piece of paper sticking out from the bottom of the refrigerator once. I knew that it was why the kitchen wasn't clean, but I refused to pick it up. I was redoing the dishes and sweeping the floor until after hours of torture, he broke down and revealed that the issue had been the piece of paper. It was a bittersweet day when he died - I was 12. My 15-

year-old sister had moved out and married a year before to get away from the 6'8 mentally ill alcoholic monster, and I had been tortured and made to feel powerless by cleaning before. This manager wouldn't break me.

Aside from raising my two younger siblings, I got my first real job when I was 15 through the Baltimore City Summer Job Corps program. I worked as a recreation aide in a nursing home on Franklin Avenue only a few blocks from the famous Edgar Allan Poe House. Working there, I learned that children born deaf, blind, or with other "deformities" were placed in nursing homes and grew up alongside the elderly. I hated the stench of death, urine, and cleaning products. I hated seeing the elderly abused by the large Black male assistants who were hired because of their strength to carry patients. When my mother was in jail, I was a junior in high school and got a job at another Murphy's store. At age 16 for minimum wage, $3.35 an hour, I pretended I was a customer and spied on potential shoplifters. I spent the summer there until I earned the one thousand dollars needed to pay for my mother's fine, which was required before she could be released after six months in jail. The summer before my senior year I also took care of the borders and kept up all the bills on the apartment building. My mother left me with bills that were three months behind. Each week, I went downtown, stood in the long line with the poor black people, and waited my turn in the crowded black run Baltimore Gas and Electric Company.

I want to make a payment on the electric bill.
Whose name is it in?
My mother, Reba Conner.

Where is she?

She is in bed. She's sick.

You need to put at least $5 down.

Okay.

Next time your mother needs to come down here herself.

Okay, can I have a receipt please?

I had that same conversation every week for six months.

Further into the broadcast, there was mention of the song "This Little Light of Mine," as Mr. Lewis used that song to lead protesters. Again, memories arose. I sang that song many times at the Helping Up Mission in West Baltimore. After school, kids in the neighborhood went there for food, clothes, toothbrushes, soap, turkeys for Thanksgiving, and maybe a special gift at Christmas time. The neighborhood children lined up perfectly straight along the fence and waited to be admitted. Only if we were all quiet and straight would the gate be unlocked.

Once I got in, I rushed to the back ballfield with all the black boys. I was chosen last to be on a team every time. I wouldn't have been chosen at all if there hadn't been a rule that everyone who wanted to play could. It certainly hurt because I usually got on base, so it wasn't because I was a bad player. My skin is white, and I am a female. This was the way things were for whites and most girls. After some time on the playground, we were rustled in to eat peanut butter and jelly sandwiches or donuts with milk or Kool-Aid, which we called bug juice. The missionaries cleaned the tables as we sat and listened to Bible stories, were taught to turn the other cheek, accept our poverty plight, and pray forgiveness for all our sins.

Another reporter mentioned Bloody Sunday. For me it was a Saturday after the media had shown the beating of Rodney King all week. I was on my way to tutor a little second grade Black boy I suspected was being abused. In a later visit, I was forced to call child protective services when the boy showed me his bruises while he was learning to read.

To get to his house, I had to drive across the city to East Baltimore. When I was almost there, I was pulled over by two Black officers who asked for my license and registration. While I nervously searched, I asked what I had done. They claimed I had been speeding and I told them that I didn't think I had been. "Shut up and give me your license," the shorter one yelled. I was terrified, shaking, and couldn't concentrate. The officers said I was taking too long and pulled me out of the car. My face was smashed into the gravel, which lined the overpass of the highway. My hands were jerked behind my back, and my wrists were handcuffed.

I could hear the cars speeding by and the familiar sound of public buses stopping and starting at red lights below the bridge. I tried to turn my head to ask what I had done to deserve this treatment but that had meant I was resisting arrest. I was also charged with speeding and assault on two police officers, but it was all a lie. My glasses were broken when my face was smashed into the gravel. My car had been towed and I was charged not only the towing fee, but a storage fee, and I barely had money to pay my rent.

I knew these two Black policemen were retaliating against me for what was happening thousands of miles away in California, the same way I had often been retaliated against for someone else's crimes, hatred, anger and ignorance. It happened in the schools, neighborhood and workplace.

As I continued watching the television reports, historian Lonnie Bunch passionately described how John Lewis worked relentlessly to create the African American Cultural Museum which he submitted a bill for every year for 20 years. Ironically, I had spent the last 8 years working to get support for a slavery museum in my town. Maybe it was because I grew up learning the importance of Black History. I was taught about George Washington Carver, Daniel Hale Williams, Fredrick Douglas, Harriet Tubman, and many other famous Black Americans, rather than about George Washington or other more commonly taught moments in United States history.

I don't recall ever learning about any white people until Mr. Chenoweth taught the Holocaust in 11th grade. This confirmed for me the importance of keeping memories alive so that people wouldn't ever forget. No, I hadn't forgotten all the harms inflicted on me by Black people and all the times I hear about my "White privilege."

In high school, there were two scholarships available: one for everyone and one for only Black people, which gave them twice the opportunity as me. I was just as poor, just as deserving, and prayed just as much in the mission every day. But why did I feel more comfortable with people of other races and cultures than what was supposedly my own?

After enough pain, being ostracized, retaliated against, abused, used, and all the other difficulties that come from growing up in poverty and/or as a minority, I no longer identified as a member of any race or group. I decided to follow the only path that ever really welcomed me, the path of universal truth—unless something was good and just for all, it wasn't good and just.

I fell in love with Native American concepts of oneness, using Great Mystery as my guide, which sometimes put me on a long, hard road, but that's what I have faith in. I believe that an injustice against one is an injustice against all. I fight for equal rights and equal access for all races, sexes and socioeconomic levels.

I have certainly been retaliated against for my efforts. I have been teaching for over 30 years and I can testify that teachers who speak up, like many good police officers, walk with a target on their backs. When I attend Black Lives Matter rallies or post social media comments of concern over the treatment of George Floyd, Elisha McClain and other victims of racism, I get complaints from white people who question my views and even my sanity. Many of these people are whites who grew up in the slum as minorities, like me, and still only see themselves as victims. They only see one type of Black person: the ones who have acted out the victimhood.

There are others, whites and Blacks, who grew up in sheltered environments and have lived under the false assumption that people who are arrested deserve it, the law and police are on the side of justice, and the "Lord" wouldn't allow otherwise.

I stand up for Black and brown minorities, the poor, the illiterate, the disenfranchised, those abused by the system, the ones left for dead, and the people with no hope. They are all parts of me. They are my experiences.

I know what it's like to be a victim of an oppressive system filled with racial injustices. If I hadn't experienced so much racial discrimination, I may not be able to identify it so easily, nor comprehend how much it exists in the world. I don't know. What I do know is that those who can't empathize with others have probably not looked deep enough inside themselves.

To see another human being as ourselves would require a painful reality check and most aren't willing to do that sort of work. It's so much easier to see the victim as the villain. After all, the pain of anger is easier than the pain of love, isn't it?

When I hear John Lewis's name, I feel a warm kinship, not because we have both been victims of racism, but because we reached the same place in our hearts and souls. I suspect Mr. Lewis believed that all people are interconnected. I would imagine that he never considered his fight as anything unique or deserving of accolades, but something that had to be done as a human being to help us evolve as one human race.

I am proud to be a part of the fight against racism because I know how damaging this assault on humanity and our planet is. I detailed many events of my life to establish the fact that I am realistic and I do know what racism feels like. I believe that unless each of us reaches into our own souls and loves ourselves fully, we will not evolve as a race. If we don't do our own work of self-love, we will continue to destroy each other's lives and ultimately the planet and human existence.

Self-love is the highest form of love and it is the only way to save the world. When we hold another in our hearts in love, we are doing the same for ourselves. When we have hate and anger in our hearts towards others, we are damaging ourselves. Self- love is the way to peace on Earth.

Are you brave enough to practice true self-love? Will you see your neighbor as yourself? Are you willing to take a step beyond the pain of anger, projection and resentment and risk it all for love?

The Necessary Metamorphosis of America

By Tiffany Redman

I used to make fun of my younger brother because he is dark-skinned. My first barbies and doll babies were all white. I adopted a common Caucasian perspective of what it meant to be beautiful. I thought because my skin-tone was lighter than my brother's, he was dirty, as were my dolls.

I am not sure my parents knew what to do about this behavior from their six-year-old daughter. I was raised in a predominantly white neighborhood. Most of the children in my school and in my extracurricular activities were white. The exposure I had to Black people came mostly from my family. My parents never taught me to hate nor allowed me to be jealous of others. My brother and I were raised on strict regimens of respect. I will never forget the day my father taught me to respect my race. He overheard me, for the hundredth time, ridicule my brother because his skin was darker than mine.

I would often make jokes about his dark complexion. During this very serious conversation, I remember my father pointing to each one of our arms and asking me what color they were. When responding to the color I saw in myself and my father, I answered brown. When it was time to identify my brother, I always said black. I used to toy with my father frequently. I was his only girl at home so I could always weasel my way out of things. Though I attempted to make light of the situation and stand firm that my brother was darker and therefore uglier, I knew my father did not appreciate my sentiments. I can still see the look of frustration he had on his face that his message was not getting through. He looked almost defeated and heartbroken.

I didn't understand his stern reaction. I thought he was just mad that I was being rude to my brother. I was young, so I do not remember how long or how many times he kept going back and forth between the three of us to get me to see that we were all the same.

I do remember the last item he used to make his point. I had a calendar that had photos of horses for each month. He pulled it off the wall and showed me the month that had a photo of three horses at the top. Two of the horses were a chocolate brown and almost the exact same color. The third horse was as black as an unlit night sky. He didn't ask me to identify their colors. He asked me if I thought they were beautiful. I, of course, told him that they were. I loved horses. I thought they all were beautiful no matter what they looked like. My father told me that I need to think of my brother and other people of color in the exact same way. That was the last day I made fun of my brother about his skin tone, however, it was not the last lesson I received about what it meant to be Black.

Years later, as a middle school student, I got made fun of by a group of teens because I "acted white." I had missed church that Sunday. When I returned to school the following week, I was told I was the topic of conversation, at that meeting. The way I spoke and acted had stripped me of my "Black card."

This was a hurdle that was hard to get over. A friend of mine had started the conversation. She was a Black girl, the same age as me, that I had known since elementary school. I didn't understand how I was "supposed" to act. I didn't understand how or why the way I acted was rejected by my peers. I didn't know any other way to act. It wasn't until I was an adult that I accepted who I was and realized that I am as black as I need to be, with or without proper grammar.

My speech doesn't stop me from getting looks at the grocery store, because I am Black. My good behavior and respect for others didn't stop a truck full of white men from yelling "nigger" out the window as I walked to work one day. My work ethic didn't change the minds of hundreds of people who didn't want "the Black girl" to ring up their groceries or take their orders, while working the many customer service jobs I had held over the years. My light-skin has never stopped the wrong type of person from looking at me like I do not deserve to be walking this earth. My light-skin has never stopped the wrong type of person from thinking my purpose would be better served if I were in chains and required to call someone master.

There isn't a single Black person alive today, or who has lived, that has not experienced racism. Many of us have turned the other cheek or accepted that this is just the way things are. Some of us do not even recognize it as racism. I am no longer able to accept this as the fate of my people. It is wrong. Racism is wrong. Prejudice is wrong. Genocide is wrong.

I am a 35-year old, Black, woman with two children. One of which is Black, the other is mixed with white. My best friends are white, the man I am currently dating is white. None of these facts change the fear I possess in my heart for my race. None of these facts have stopped me from wanting to find a way to take every single Black person and keep them in my pocket so that I may try to protect them.

Truth be told, I have never had a preference in who I date until last year. I have always dated men of all races. This can obviously be seen in the ethnicities of my children. Last year, I went on a mission to find a Black man for a mate. I thought if I could find just one Black man, I could keep him safe. I could take on the responsibility of protecting him from the world.

This decision was hard to deter from as my current partner is not Black. My multicultural lifestyle only allows me to see the destruction of a race that many seem not to care about. Also, I ultimately see the separation and demise of our country, if prejudice and racism remain the status quo.

I am also what most people would call an empath. I don't particularly like labels, however, this one fits me for sure. I genuinely love and care for everyone on this earth. I don't always like that this is the way I am wired but it is so.

My parents raised me to be respectful, but God gets all the credit for how my heart beats and the way my mind thinks. I can feel people's pain no matter what they are going through. People gravitate towards me for support on a regular basis. Strangers have told me their darkest secrets that I have kept to this day. I whole-heartedly believe in love, respect, and I believe that we as humans have an obligation to purposefully take care of one another.

I realize that everyone doesn't have the same heart as me. I know that people aren't openly vulnerable to others. I also know basic human decency is not a quality that only I possess. The very thing that makes humans different from animals is the ability to care for one another. Animals look out for those that are in the same species. How are humans one of the largest and only civilized species but do not exhibit this behavior? I believe it is necessary for the betterment of society to practice the cliché phrase, "It takes a village." Our village is burning. Our village is under attack. Our village is no longer a village.

I watched a video of a Black man that died on May 25, 2020 at the hands of a White police officer. It is positively disgusting to say that this sequence of events is not unknown to American history. I watched the video on May 26, 2020. I didn't watch the 10 second news clips. I didn't find out what happened from a tasteless, social media meme. I watched the entire 10-minute video of a man who was alive at the beginning and dead at the end. I watched the seven or so people surrounding the scene, pleading with the officer to remove his knee from this man's neck. I heard the desperation in the voices of the witnesses when they demanded someone check this man's pulse. I watched the careless looks on the faces of the officers who participated in taking this man's life.

Again, these things happen in America. It wasn't the death of George Floyd that caused me to suddenly care about the repeated mistreatment of Black people. It was the death of George Floyd that broke my spirit in ways I didn't know it could bend. It was the death of George Floyd that made me remember Sandra Bland. It was the death of George Floyd that made me remember Travon Martin. Two weeks before George Floyd was murdered, two other persons of color were also unjustly killed. Within two weeks after George Floyd was murdered, there were reports of Black people hanging from trees and more unlawful deaths at the hands of law enforcement.

These are not to even count the many who died, before this murder in May 2020, for no other reason than the color of their skin. My daughter's birthday was May 27, 2020. I am not sure what I did the night after I watched the video of this man dying. I may have been in a mindset due to working my normal Tuesday evening shift and didn't have much time to reflect on what I had just seen at that moment. I remember exactly how the next day went. I spent the entire day crying and asking myself why things are this way. I had to stop myself from being upset so I could successfully prepare for my daughter's birthday celebrations.

I remember calling my brother and begging him to be safe. He is a Black man living in America, so when something happens he is my first thought. I just wanted to remind him to be safe. I wanted to remind him that I love him. I wanted him to know that he has support and his life matters. I called my mother. I cried. I told her how unfair it was. I asked her why we are treated differently. I asked her what right people have to wish for our demise and display hatred so openly. I hysterically carried on as I could not calm myself. I asked her how her generation lived through this.

My mother was born in 1961. This was 100 years after slavery had ended, yet it was in the middle of the years that America deemed the Black person a threat. I thought about the issues I've dealt with and realized it was a hundred times worse when she was growing up. Racism is a Rubik's cube to me. I understand people are conditioned with generational influence. What I don't understand is those same people not acknowledging that the influence is wrong.

As someone who feeds off the feelings and emotions of others, the climate our world is in and has experienced baffles me. I do not understand it. I do not understand why I am a threat because I am Black. I do not understand why I am labeled as worthless. I do not understand why the color of my skin means I cannot be trusted. I do not understand why my Black heritage prevents me from being treated as the equal I am. I do not understand why in the year 2020 my race is still held with such small regard. I do not understand why our cities are the first to be forgotten. I do not understand why our culture is copied but not appreciated. I do not understand why our children must be taught at such a young age to keep the chains of our ancestors close by, as to not encourage further injury.

I also refuse to accept it. My mother, father, and stepfather accepted it. My grandparents accepted it. The Blacks who were enslaved accepted it. Those who died on a tree hundreds of years ago accepted it. Black people have lived in fear all their lives, in America.

I ask white-America, what are you so afraid of? If we are weak, what is there to fear? If we are uneducated, what is there to fear? If we are incapable, what is there to fear? These stereotypes are the fabricated reasons that help too many people sleep at night. These illusions bring some peace as they treat us as animals.

The one laughable thing about this whole mess is all the contradictions. There are no real answers to these questions because they are lies. They are the blanket of deceit placed into the white man's mind. We are nowhere near weak, incapable, or uneducated. I feel as though I'm not saying anything that isn't already known. Most only fear what they do not understand. We can be of no threat if we are not of great value. It is understood exactly how capable we are. Fear of the person isn't the issue, it is fear of our greatness. It is an attempt to procure a dominant race. This is a time of great reckoning. We are tired of being pushed around. We are tired of being silent. We are entitled to every bit of freedom as any other ethnicity in this world. We deserve the respect that all humans are due. There is not a reason that will ever justify the treatment of the Black race.

No matter where you place your marker in history, it will not be a time when Black people were thought of and treated as equals. America prides herself on being the land of the free and the home of the brave. Where can we be free? Where can we be brave? Our lawmakers, leaders, and law enforcers have gotten too comfortable with pushing us to the side and putting us under the ground. They have had too much peace while we shed blood. We deserve our seat at the table. We deserve to be heard. We deserve to be equal. We deserve what is fair.

America needs a complete reconstruction. The laws that are in place do not effectively protect people of color. There are still clauses within the declaration of independence that create exceptions for one's freedoms. We need to be sure that no form of slavery is ever allowed in America, that includes extreme jail sentences for people color. Any person who commits crimes against a person solely because of their appearance needs to be brought to justice. This includes police officers who abuse their power.

I do not want to be American if it means I must continue walking with my head down. I do not want to be American if my children, nieces, and nephews are made targets at birth. I will not be this American. I have been this American my entire life. I deserve better. My family and friends deserve better. We all deserve better.

Now is the time that I chose to take an active role in my future and in the future of my community. I cannot only pray that things will get better. I must put forth the effort, energy, and encouragement to place my community in a better position.

Someone called me an activist recently. I wasn't sure I wanted the title because I didn't want to be associated with only the movement for Black people. As I thought about where I am in life, the type of person I am, and what I want for the world; I realized I am an activist for all.

One of the first things on my list to tackle is protection for Black people. Others can continue to be racist, and prejudice, and wish us harm. By the time we are finished, all anyone who wants to harm us will be able to do is wish it.

One Love Fits All

By Dawn Rix

As I drive through the hills of West Virginia and cross the Harpers Ferry bridge where the Potomac and Shenandoah Rivers meet, I look up at the sun and think about the diversity of my state.

It's hard to believe there was a time when the Hatfield's and McCoy's existed! There was a rumor that if someone was anything other than a white man, he would not drive up the mountain for fear he may not come home. Today, people often pretend the Ku Klux Klan and similar domestic terrorist groups did not exist. They did and still do.

It is sad that with so much division in the world, people often sit behind their computer screens and have the nerve to share hateful opinions. Social media is full of crude comments, uneducated opinions, and fake news. It is seemingly just full-blown negativity and hatred. I have watched my computer screen as two of my friends who grew up together, played basketball together, ate dinner together, hung out together, and who had each other's backs like inseparable brothers were now at war. Each response was cutthroat and insulting. So much hatred was being poured from their hearts. I almost felt like it was fueled by outside sources. It was truly heartbreaking watching their exchange. They were family. They never seemed to have thought of each other's skin tone but now they were accusing one another of being "racist pigs."

It got ugly as they began their threats, telling each other what they would do if they saw the other out in town. I know racism exists now but as a child I was oblivious to it. I grew up in a subdivision that primarily was made up of all whites except for one family: the See family. We loved them. Their home was our safe place. As kids, we ran the neighborhood fearlessly with not a worry or care in the world.

The rule was that once the streetlight came on, it was time to go home. It often didn't matter which home because we were a tight knit community and everyone was always welcome in any of the homes. We were always cooking out, playing kickball, staying over even on weeknights, and walking to school together in the morning. I was surprised a few years later, after returning from Maryland, on my first day at a new school when I was confronted by a dark-skinned girl demanding that I "go back where I came from!" I was shocked and in tears until another girl stood up and told her to sit down and leave me alone. That girl instantly became my hero.

A few months later we had a school dance that was held at the local Lion's Club. I was excited to attend because I loved to dance and be social with my friends. The place was decorated nicely, the records were spinning, and the music was thumping as I made my way straight to the dance floor. I was in my zone, pulling out all my dance moves, when suddenly the song skipped and it went silent. We all froze. This was my scariest childhood memory. Our dee jay, who was in the 6th grade, but 6-feet tall, announced to everyone to blame the white girl for the record skipping. As I stood in the middle of the dance floor, I slowly looked around to see who that was. All eyes were staring back at me! The moment was devastating. I didn't understand

and left in tears, dreading the upcoming school days where I would be known as "that girl."

Needless-to-say, I survived. Later, at a different school, I met the woman who would later become my ultimate role model: the late Mary T. Doakes, my junior high school principal. She was the very best. She was tough and ran a tight ship. She would jack you up and did not give a crap if you were white as snow or black as an ace of spades. It did not matter. She would tell us straight up she expected more out of us. That was her thing. She was a strong, proud, Black woman and did not hesitate to tell you about yourself.

No matter what color they were, if she found students sneaking out to smoke or skipping school, it was guaranteed that she would snatch them up by the shirt and they would never do it again.

She also built us up and gave solid chances. She told us like it was but treated everyone with fairness and respect. When it comes to discipline and punishment, I think sometimes children don't understand that adults are doing things *for* them, not *to* them. I think Ms. Doakes telling us she was disappointed in us was more of a punishment than any lecture, office visit, or detention. If we saw her walking up the hallway with a ruler stick, we knew we best be walking the line. All she had to do was look at us. She taught us about being accountable, taking responsibility, and that for every decision we made or action we took, there would be a consequence to follow, so we must choose wisely.

One of the wisest choices I made was to get involved in extracurricular activities to meet new people. We shared the same night-time rituals, ate the same breakfast, and never paid attention to our skin tones. We were bonded by friendships and our commonalities. We were kids who played together, laughed together, and sang together.

I was in a show choir made up of multiple nationalities. There, we were only separated by altos, tenors, bass and sopranos. It didn't matter what our race was. We had multi-community events and fundraisers. We were known for our delicious sub sales and all of us had hands in making, wrapping, and delivering them. Buyers had no concern about who prepared the food and quite frankly could care less, as long as it tasted good.

One evening after one of our famous sub sales, my mom got a phone call from my sister in Baltimore. This was not just an ordinary phone call; this one was different. Very different. She told my mother to sit down.

My mom was a worrier and responded, "Oh dear lord Sharon, what?"

Sharon was getting married. The relief on my mom's face was priceless.

"Mom there is something else you need to know." She continued, "He is your age."

"Okay," my mother replied again.

"And mom," she paused. "He is Black!"

My mom almost dropped the phone in shock. She said, "Oh my Sharon…. Give me a minute to take all this in."

My mom was not prejudiced, she just wanted her girls to find love and be treated like a lady should be. Although she appeared to be a bit startled, she was ready and willing to welcome him with open arms but told my sister it was not going to be easy for her.

The happy couple was married and attended several jazz festivals and art exhibits. My sister loved socializing and having fun, until one night at a concert hall she was approached by a Black woman who scolded her and asked her who she thought she was, being with a Black man. She told her she "Needed to stick with her own kind." How dare she steal a good Black man from good Black women?

My sister was in shock and learned quickly that acts of racism do not discriminate but people do.

My best guy friend and I were aware of this when we considered dating. We both knew it was taboo, would probably stir up a lot of talk, and we would get a lot of backlash if we ever were to go out. As disappointing as it was, we mutually agreed it would be best at that time to strictly remain just friends. We respected and adored one another. We had a strong connection and built a friendship based on shared ambitions, goals, and dreams. We made a promise to one another. He was going to play for the NFL, and I was going to pursue becoming a big country music singer and superstar.

Several years later I was working in a busy hair salon and got a phone call. The receptionist knew I was busy, and that she should just take a message. Instead, she interrupted to tell me the call was coming from Dallas. I put down my shears and made a beeline to the phone. Much to my surprise it was him. He wanted me to be the first to hear from him as his team walked out onto the field of the Texas AT&T Stadium to play for the first time. I was beyond excited for him.

He then married and had kids, and I recorded some music, married, and had children of my own. A few years later when he made it back home, we reconnected as adults and divorced parents. This time the world was more accepting, and we could go out on dates with no permission needed and no second thoughts. We were just two people who kept a promise to stay connected and grown teenagers who lived out their dreams. We walked in and out of places together proudly, sometimes hand in hand with no hesitation, and I opened my home to him and his children for a short period of time.

When my daughter was growing up, her very best friend was a dark-skinned Black girl. Every year we would go to the beach for vacation and they would walk the boardwalk with cornrows in their hair. I never second-guessed her staying over or if the house my daughter was visiting was clean. I never wondered if they were eating right or being treated properly. I never had a thought of what family members were there. They were best friends that did not call for approval of others.

I believe in individual accountability. I believe we must know when we need to take a stand for what we believe in. I believe we all have a voice that needs to be heard. I believe people should think out of the box and learn from each other. After all, you don't know what you don't know!

That saying carried on to my days as a salon owner. I had a full-service salon with several employees. One of my main stylists was and still is the best natural hair stylist. When a former salon owner with a senior clientele came to me for a job, that same natural hair stylist wanted no part in it. She considered quitting if I hired the other stylist because there were rumors that she was prejudiced and had said nasty things about Black people in the past. We didn't want that. I still needed to make a fair decision as a business owner whether or not to turn this person away or give her an opportunity to prove gossipers wrong. It had never been my policy to turn people away. I had an open-door policy. My staff consisted of people who were gay, straight, Black, and white. It did not matter. I spoke to both ladies individually and reassured my stylist there would be no tolerance for racist remarks.

What I did next was a risky move. I could have separated them and had them work different shifts. Instead, I made them work together. At first there was a bit of tension and uncertainty. It was an adjustment for them and their clients.

Over time, the former salon owner with the older clientele got used to being around everyone and began welcoming my stylists' Thursday and Friday appointments with fresh coffee and snacks. Soon it was just a room of women getting their hair done, sharing stories, and laughing while enjoying their visit without it mattering what color their skin was. Before long both stylists became friends. I never thought it would work out as well as it did, but it just goes to show again, people don't know what they don't know.

When I was at basic training, there were 30 women from many backgrounds thrown together. We had a stripper, a rich girl, a pastor's daughter, a Black girl from Georgia, a Christian, an atheist, a Vietnamese woman, an Arkansas country girl, a beauty school graduate, and many more. We were stripped of any bit of self-worth we had. We were taught to adapt and overcome. We had to learn about one another and accept and put aside our differences. Our focus was on becoming airwomen for the United States Air force. All prejudging and stereotyping no longer existed. Over the course of six weeks in training, we cried together, prayed together, and marched together.

During our final physical training exercises, the country girl fell back exhausted and said she couldn't do it, ready to give up. She was in tears, but we refused to let her quit. Never leaving anyone behind, we ran back, locked arms and carried her to the finish line where as one solid unit we were then awarded Honor Flight.

We can unite despite how diverse we are. We don't know what we don't know, and we have a responsibility to ourselves to each other to open our eyes, ears, mind and heart to learn.

I believe people have more in common than they do not, from the fairest of porcelain skin to the darkest ebony, all tones on the spectrum of skin color are equally beautiful. We all live and die. We all bleed the same. We need to stay focused on individual accountability. It is easier said than done but we are each accountable for our own thoughts and decisions and must try to make things better. We are so much more alike than we are different.

As the lyrics in my new song say:

How bad does it have to get?

How many have to fall,

before we make this world

where one love fits all?

A Change is Gonna Come… I Hope

By Shannon Robinson

I was a student at Powhatan Elementary School in Baltimore County, where there were not many little girls that looked like me. I was tall and lanky with black skin and brown eyes. My hair was long and braided. My mother spent hours every weekend braiding my hair so that she would not have to tackle it during the week.

All the girls I played with at my elementary school, including my best friend at the time, were white. They all had long flowing blonde hair, blue eyes, and flawless skin, and I wanted to look like them. I hated always being the tallest. I didn't like my black skin. I wanted my eyes to look like the sky. And I wanted my hair to cascade down my back and bounce while I was playing.

When I was six years old, I came home after school one day and announced to my mother that I wanted to be white. I proudly walked into the kitchen where she was preparing dinner and made this stunning announcement, "Mommy, I want to be white."

My mother, probably never thinking she would have to have this conversation with her Black daughter, stopped what she was doing and gazed reflectively at my sweet innocent brown face. "Why do you want to be white?" my mother asked. I quickly and matter-of-factly replied, "Because white girls are pretty. Their skin is pretty. They have eyes that look like the sky. And their hair is long and bounces when they run."

I am not sure if the look on my mother's face was one of sadness, disappointment, or anger but it was obvious that my proclamation shocked her. My mother wiped her hands on the kitchen towel and led me into the living room where we sat on the sofa, with me on her lap. She paused and looked into my brown eyes for a few moments. She gently traced the outline of my face, my nose, and my lips with her finger. She played in my neatly braided hair that hung to my shoulders with the pretty red bows on the end of each braid, and then in a gentle and loving tone said, "Baby girl, you cannot be white."

My bottom lip began to tremble, and I could feel the tears welling up in my eyes. With a quivering voice and my eyes looking towards the floor, I said, "But why?" My mother lifted my chin, kissed me on my nose, and said, "Because God made you a Black princess, and Black is beautiful."

It would be many years later before I would discover that the innocent conversation with my mother was a pain point for her.

It was Thanksgiving 1988, and I was home on leave from the military. My mother and my dad were putting the finishing touches on what was sure to be a scrumptious Thanksgiving feast of perfectly roasted duck, glazed ham, my mother's famous potato salad, baked macaroni and cheese, candied yams, collard greens, string beans, and cornbread. There was enough food for a small army, however, it would only be my immediate family, and my brother's new girlfriend Susan. My dad had met Susan prior to Thanksgiving and only shared that she was a nice young lady. My mother and I were anxious to meet her so we could drill her with questions, which was standard practice for anyone dating my brother.

My brother and Susan arrived promptly at 4 pm. My dad was sitting in the living room as my brother and Susan entered the apartment. I was in the dining room preparing the table to be set, and my mother was in the kitchen getting the good dishes out of the cabinet. My dad and I greeted Susan warmly and welcomed her to our home. My mother came into the dining room from the kitchen just as my brother was removing Susan's coat and stopped dead in her tracks. My brother proceeded to introduce Susan to my mother. Susan, obviously very excited about meeting my mother, said "It is so good to finally meet you!" My mother, however, did not say a word. She merely stood there, holding the dishes, with a look of disgust on her face. For what seemed like ten long minutes, my mother said absolutely nothing, not one word, and then she broke her silence by looking at my brother and saying, "That girl is not welcomed in my home!"

I was stunned, shocked, and speechless. My mother aggressively placed the dishes she had been holding on the table and went to her bedroom which was in the rear of our apartment. The air in the home was thick with tension, and none of us knew exactly what to do or say at that moment. My brother, clearly embarrassed and angry, decided it wasn't worth the fight. He and Susan left without eating dinner. I looked at my dad and he said, "I knew that wasn't going to go over well."

I was still trying to figure out what just happened. Did my mother know Susan? Had they had a negative encounter before? I needed answers so I went to the source: my mother.

The door to my parent's bedroom was closed. I knocked and waited for my mother to say come in. When I entered the room, my mother was sitting on the side of the bed with a look of anger that I don't think I had ever seen before. I asked if she was ok and she asked, "Are they gone?"

I said, "Yes they are, but what was that? Why did you say Susan could not sit at your table?"

My mother replied, "Because she is white."

I sat on the side of my mother's bed and stared at her with a look of surprise on my face. "Why?" I asked. It was then that I learned that my mother did not particularly care for white people.

My mother was born in 1944 and grew up in the south during the 1950s and 60s. She encountered discrimination, racism, prejudice, and other social injustices against Black people firsthand. If that was not enough, my mother told me the story of how a white woman accused my dad of rape, a crime he did not commit but spent time in jail for. Admittedly, I was troubled by what I was hearing.

This was the storyline of a movie. Or the plot of a book. Not something that happened in my family. As I tried to digest what I had just heard, I thought of Emmett Till, a 14-year-old boy that was murdered by a group of white men for allegedly flirting with a white woman. I was blindsided at my mother's startling revelation because, in spite of her personal experiences and beliefs, it did not affect how she raised my brother and me. I never had the opportunity to ask my mother if it was difficult for her not to pass her feelings and beliefs on to her children but I respected her for giving my brother and me the freedom to love people for who they are.

My experiences of wanting to be white as a child, learning about my mother's own experiences of racism and how they shaped her, as well as hearing the story of my dad being falsely accused by a white woman of rape, affected me in ways later in life that I could not even fathom. Interestingly enough, I had not yet had my own run-in with racism but that would change in 1999.

I was in my twelfth year of service in the Air Force when I decided to cross-train into a different career field. The switch from Information Management Specialist to Education & Training Manager required me to attend a six-week school at Sheppard Air Force Base in Wichita Falls, Texas.

There were approximately 20 students in the class with me and bonds were instantly formed. Because we were away from home during Thanksgiving, eight of us, four men and four women, decided to drive to New Mexico for the long holiday weekend. We rented two cars, with the men in one car and the women in the other.

The drive to New Mexico started out unscenic and uneventful. The route we mapped out was flat farmland, not much to see at all, but the women were having a great time singing and laughing, so the lack of scenery did not bother us much. About two hours into the drive, a bathroom break was requested. We made a telephone call to the men asking them to take the next exit with a bathroom. The restaurant we found was a hole in the wall and quite noticeably in a pretty desolate area. Besides a gas station across the road, there were no other businesses or people around. There weren't many cars in the parking lot of the restaurant and I wasn't feeling real comfortable but the sound of music and people laughing coming from inside the restaurant put me at ease….a little.

When our eight Black faces walked into the restaurant, it became crystal clear rather quickly that we were not welcome. It was as though E.F. Hutton himself had walked in. The laughing and talking that we heard when we were outside stopped. Every person in the restaurant was now glaring at us in a rather frightening kind of way. The only sound was the jukebox blaring the Dixie Chicks, singing "Cowboy Take Me Away." A quick scan of the restaurant confirmed what I had suspected, we were the only Black faces in the place. The quick change in the atmosphere inside the restaurant let me know that our Black faces walking into the restaurant was not expected and dare I say, not wanted.

After what seemed like a very long time, an older white woman with gray hair and a deep raspy voice said, "May I help you?" My overeager, extroverted, love-everyone friend, Cee-Cee, began to enthusiastically tell the woman that we were traveling to New Mexico and wanted to use the restroom.

The woman, as well as every other person in the restaurant, glared at us and then said, "You're not from around these parts are you?"

Cee-Cee, oblivious to the tension in the air, told the woman that we are in the military temporarily stationed at Sheppard Air Force Base. The woman, totally ignoring everything that Cee-Cee was saying replied, "And you're not going to be here long, are you?"

The seven of us knew that was our cue to leave immediately. Cee-Cee, however, was a little slower to grasp the subtle message of, "You are not wanted here." I grabbed Cee-Cee by her arm and we got out of there in a hurry. I was frightened, shocked, and angry that in 1999 I would not be welcome somewhere because of the color of my skin. Although the woman did not specifically say we were not welcomed because we were Black, her tone and words made it quite obvious.

Even though I was frightened, shocked, and angry, I was equally not interested in demanding to use the restroom. We got into our vehicles and left, thankful to be alive. That was the last time I would experience racism personally but as a Black woman living in these yet-to-be United States, the racism and social injustices that Black people still face is very much felt.

No one ever imagined that when we said "Happy New Year," sang Auld Lang Syne, and kissed our loved ones on January 1, 2020, that it would be the year that we wish we could forget. Aside from the sudden and tragic death of Kobe Bryant, wildfires and a pandemic, the murders of Ahmaud Arbery, Breonna Taylor, George Floyd, and Rayshard Brooks by white police officers has shaken this country to its core.

Protests, riots, and looting broke out not only in the United States but in other parts of the world as well. The hashtag "Black Lives Matter" is trending again. Racist friends, followers, and colleagues are being exposed by their social media posts and comments, regarding the Black Lives Matter movement and the murder of George Floyd in particular. Black people are angry, and mentally and emotionally exhausted, and we have every reason to be.

The murders of Ahmaud, Breonna, George, and Rayshard brought to the surface the stories my mother told me of her own experiences with racism. I've thought about my dad being falsely accused of the rape of a white woman. I've thought about Atatiana Jefferson, Stephon Clark, Aura Rosser, Trayvon Martin, Botham Jean, Philando Castille, Alton Sterling, Freddie Gray, Sandra Bland, Eric Garner, Tamir Rice, and countless others who have been murdered by white people. I think of Kalief Browder and the Central Park 5 (Kevin Richardson, Raymand Santana, Antron McCray, Yusef Salaam, and Korey Wise), and the horrors they faced simply because of the color of their skin. I get mad at the stories of white men and women that are calling the police on black people, making false reports that they "feared for their lives." We are experiencing modern lynching and the Ku Klux Klan are now wearing uniforms that swore to protect and serve. Enough is enough.

Christians will say that we don't have a racism problem, we have a heart problem. White people fail to recognize their privilege or choose to live in denial. White friends comfort themselves by convincing themselves that they "Don't see color," and want me and other Black people to help them understand or make them feel better. Who will make *us* feel better? Who will protest with *us*? Who will fight with *us*? Who will speak up for *us*? At this point in my life, I am no longer interested in comforting anyone that fails to see and or understand that we have a serious problem in this country.

I can no longer accept silence in the wake of Black people being murdered by white people. Silence speaks volumes as to where a person stands and at this point in the game, a person is either an ally or a foe. No longer can people hide behind the guise of comfortability. No longer can white people straddle the fence. Now is the time to choose and take a stand.

I must continue to be vocal about the social injustices in our country for my nieces and nephews, and the next generation as a whole. It would be a tragedy for our children to have the same conversations that we are having now; the same conversations that our parents and grandparents had.

I feel that my generation dropped the ball and I wish I knew why. However, gone are the days of excuses. It is time for myself and others to use our voices and stand in our truth. The truth is that this country was built on the backs of Black people. The truth is that the system was designed to keep Black people down. The truth is that we not only have a heart problem, we also have a system problem.

To quote Ta-Nehisi Coates, when asked if he had reason to hope that racism in America will one day change:

Slavery in this country was 250 years. What that means is that there were African Americans who were born in this country in 1750/1760 and if they looked backward their parents were slaves. Their grandparents were slaves. Their great grandparents were slaves. If they looked forward, their children would be slaves. Their grandchildren would be slaves. Their grandchildren would be slaves. And possibly, their great-grandchildren will be slaves. There was no real hope within their individual life span of ending enslavement-the most brutal form of degradation in this country's history. There was nothing in their life that said, "This will end in my lifetime. I will see the end of this" And they struggled. And they resisted.

I don't know if I will see change in my lifetime. I hold on to hope that we as a nation will begin to move in the right direction to ensure equality for all. But what I do know for sure is that I will continue to speak out against the systemic oppression that has plagued Black people for far too long.

There been times that I thought I wouldn't last for long. Now I think I'm able to carry on. It's been a long, a long time coming. But I know a change's gonna come, oh, yes, it will...Sam Cooke, A Change's Gonna Come

Well Done, RBG

This book had already been sent to the be formatted, when I got the word of Supreme Court Justice, Ruth Bader Ginsburg's passing. Immediately I went to the Facebook group page with all our contributors and let them know I would be pulling it back. There was no way I would allow this book to be published without paying her the distinct honor she deserves.

As I sat down to begin writing, my mind went back to the day that I watched admirers from around the country drop to do pushups on courthouse steps around the country in celebration of Justice Bader Ginsburg's 86th birthday. Push-ups were her signature. What a way to celebrate the Super Diva's born day.

I then put my laptop aside and sent a message to some friends and colleagues, "Let's drop and do ten push-ups of our own." I laughed out loud when I got the response from my friend Toni in California, "What the hell? Who is going to get me up off the floor once I get down there?" I have not done push-ups in about 30 years. I could certainly relate. I was not sure I could even do three of them but for some reason I felt compelled to try and I did.

I still marvel at the uniqueness of our new generation. Only they would come up with such a celebration for "The Notorious RBG," as some affectionally call the Supreme Court justice. They understood the power she possessed, how determined she was and how hard she fought for women's rights and equality.

Before even donning her first black robe as a judge, Justice Ginsburg brought about a small revolution in how women were treated by wiping hundreds of laws that discriminated off the books. Over decades to follow, first as an Appeals Court Judge and then as the second woman on the Supreme Court, she would become to women what Thurgood Marshall was to African Americans.

On September 18, 2020, a very sad and devastating day for America, Associate Justice Ginsburg died at the age of 87 due to complications from metastatic pancreatic cancer.

What would we do without her? How far would women be set back now? Would the current administration go against her wishes and fill her seat before the upcoming election?

I did not know the answer to the first two questions, but there was no doubt in my mind that the later would happen somehow. Even though the same opportunity was denied to President Barack Obama in 2016, the current administration would move forward in filling the vacancy, going against Associate Justice Ginsburg's dying wish. No justice in history has been confirmed later than July before a presidential election, yet there was no doubt in my mind that 2020 will be the exception.

What I also knew is that I could not write about Ruth Bader Ginsburg without including Layne Diehl, another contributor to this anthology. Layne's life carries so many similarities as the Associate Justice. Even when fighting her own personal battles, Layne fights tirelessly for the betterment of others. The words that follow are her tribute.

"Rosh hashana marks the beginning of the Jewish new year, a time for reflection and introspection. Many in the Jewish community have suggested that the death of Ruth Bader Ginsburg during this time is significant as marking the life of a person of great righteousness. The period precedes Yom Kippur, a day of atonement.

How equally appropriate a time to honor a woman who dedicated her life's work to dismantling discrimination. In her honor, may we all come to atone for our nation's indiscretion of denying its promise of equal justice for all.

I am unaware of a woman in the practice of law who does not have admiration for Justice Ginsburg. Every female colleague I know, and an overwhelming majority of my male colleagues as well, respects her regardless of political affiliation. She set the example for a practice of integrity, courage, and a fierceful grace. Her name has become synonymous with the word notorious. She was a humble warrior whose use of the pen seized the sword from the grasp of the oppressor rendering it defenseless.

She was known as much for her dissents as she was for her majority opinions. Her words on the issue of dissention are an inspiration to all who struggle for justice. She says, "Dissents speak to a future age. It's not simply to say, 'My colleagues are wrong, and I would do it this way.' But the greatest dissents do become court opinions and gradually over time their views become the dominant view. So that's the dissenter's hope: that they are writing not for today, but for tomorrow."

In the brief hours that have passed since her death, I have seen many posts stating, "May her memory be a revolution." I couldn't agree more. So, to all my sisters out there who dissent, and to my brothers too, I implore you, dissent with the determination of Ruth Bader Ginsberg. Have faith that revolution is immanent. Speak life into the future of our children so that they may come to know a more perfect union, the one that lives up to its promise."….Layne Diehl

Epilogue

By Teresa Holmes

As I prepared to settle down and write this closing, I took a few minutes to chat with my youngest brother, Ray, who has lent his ear and shoulder to me throughout this book writing process.

The gist of our conversation is the expectation of our readers. "We want to immerse ourselves in the powerful stories of the struggle. We never know what someone has been through or is going through. What better way than to hear their stories? Each should be unique with some common elements."

My brother's words brought me to tears. I had just had a similar conversation with Ally, our amazing editor, not two minutes before speaking with him.

The contributors in this book are of varying ages and ethnicities. We all shared different experiences and perspectives on divisive issues, but the mission for each is identical.

We will not be bystanders. We will be catalysts for change and help to create space for growth, understanding and healing. We have each pledged solidarity in taking steps forward to cultivate meaningful transformation.

This cannot stop with us. We need you in the fight with us. This is a time to not only listen to the experiences of others but is also a time for action.

There is power in coming together. We cannot remain silent or stagnant. We must prepare ourselves for the honest, vulnerable and crucial conversations ahead, and do whatever it takes to move forward.

Let us be Boots on the Ground moving forward. Inaction should no longer be an option. Even if imperfect, action rooted in love and taken to support a social cause, is better than no action at all.

Let us be Boots on the Ground.